ROOSEVELT

—And Then?

✫

"And it ought to be remembered that there is nothing more difficult to take in hand, more perilous to conduct, or more uncertain in its success, than to take the lead in the introduction of a new order of things."

—Niccolò Machiavelli
"The Prince."

ROOSEVELT
—*And Then?*

BY
STANLEY HIGH

HARPER & BROTHERS PUBLISHERS

NEW YORK AND LONDON
1937

CONTENTS

★

ROOSEVELT

—And Then?

★

CHAPTER I

"THE PRESIDENT!"

IT IS quite likely that what Franklin D. Roosevelt did
will fill fewer pages in history than what he started.
He has been hailed as the Messiah of the New Order.
He may be only its John the Baptist. He has created an
atmosphere, released forces and set a trend in the
United States which are as much more significant than
the New Deal as they are beyond its control. Their curse
or blessing will be upon the land long after Mr. Roosevelt, at some future inaugural, has moved over to give
the right hand seat in the White House car to his
successor.

How much they will be curse and how much blessing
it is too soon to say. That is a problem, not for the chil-
dren, but for the grandchildren of the New Deal. Very
few Presidents will be judged as little as Mr. Roosevelt
in terms of what they put their names to while in office.
Future Presidents, for a good many quadrennia, are
likely to be engaged, as the case may be, building on

[1]

his foundations or extricating the nation from his bog. Whichever they are doing none of them will be in any doubt as to whom they are indebted for the need to do it. Mr. Roosevelt may or may not occupy the White House after 1940. But the consequences of Mr. Roosevelt are sure to occupy the man who does.

Mr. Roosevelt may not have started out in public life to be President. There is some evidence that it was Mrs. Roosevelt who started for him. But once President, it was certain that he would never be content to be numbered merely as one of the Presidents. He was sure to aim to be one of the great Presidents. In that he was fortunate. The 1933 crisis did for him and his place in history what it has usually taken a war to do for other Presidents. If he had met that crisis and let it go at that he would have stood, if not above, at least head and shoulders with any other peace-time President. Even his enemies will agree, I think, that he met the crisis. And his friends admit—some of them in sorrow—that he has not let it go at that. Like Woodrow Wilson, the way in which he waged the war is being eclipsed by the way in which he is waging peace.

He may have more, or less, success than Wilson had. But his risk, like Wilson's, is of his own making. Beginning in 1935, when the economic tide had turned, he could have begun the progressive demobilization of the New Deal. He would have been elected just as handily in 1936. His biggest 1936 assets were recovery and the Republicans. Moreover, had he demobilized the New Deal, the "Era of Good Feeling" which, in the weariness of the last days of the campaign, he seemed genuinely anxious to establish, might have come to pass. He could have been a recovery President and, during these four years, coasted comfortably to his place in history.

But he chose otherwise. The only New Deal demobilization to date has been brought about, not by executive order, but by the Supreme Court. The President's policy toward the Supreme Court is proof enough that, far from seeking to escape or modify the long-time consequences of the New Deal, he accepts and is determined to increase and intensify them. He is the maker of those consequences. The question is: how far is he aware of them, does he understand them and, in the phraseology of his Madison Square Garden speech, will he be their master?

It is hard to believe that he is unaware of them. Despite the minds through which most of his information is filtered before it gets to him and the unwillingness of anyone to appear, very frequently at least, as the bearer of bad tidings, he can hardly escape the fact that since his second inauguration Washington has been in a political ferment that has gone increasingly sour. Congress is no longer his echo chamber as it once was. His policies have brought a division in his own party between those who want to go on and those who want to

[3]

go back which will tax even his great capacity as a bridger of gulfs. These things are too obvious to be missed even inside the insulation of the White House.

It is hard to believe, too, that he is unaware of the fact that these Washington phenomena are not merely indicative of the perversity of politicians. They are signs of the times. It is too soon to say that the New Deal may turn out to be only a house of cards. But it is not too soon to say that the forces to the right and left of the New Deal—which put Mr. Roosevelt in office in 1932 and kept him there in 1936—have finally fallen out. It is altogether unlikely that they will ever fall in again. Conservatives—who have swallowed their conservatism and aided Mr. Roosevelt—are turning conservative again. And the latter state of their conservatism is likely to be more hidebound than the former. Liberals—who took Mr. Roosevelt's half loaf as preferable to none— are out to get the other half. And beyond established party lines, forces which Mr. Roosevelt shook out of their lethargy, made into a fighting unit and accustomed to the smell of gunpowder and the loot of war the dispossessed, the workers, farmers, white collar liberals "have only just begun to fight." Their fighting will be less and less for Mr. Roosevelt and at his direction and more and more through their own political organizations and for themselves.

The President is too accurate an observer to be unaware of these things. And he is too good a politician to overlook the fact that once it is finally determined that he is not to be the candidate in 1940 his most potent hold upon his own party organization will be measurably loosened and the danger of New Deal disintegration rapidly increased.

It is not so easy to say how far his understanding goes. Even though he is aware of all that is on the way, up to the present he has not had to meet it. And the first fact about the Roosevelt understanding is that it is better in action than in anticipation. It is dependent, not so much upon mental discipline as upon external conditions. I do not believe that he gives much thought to troubles in prospect. He waits for them to arrive. Until they do arrive he is likely to be indifferent to them and impatient of anyone who persists in bringing them to his attention. He thoroughly dislikes alarmists and prophets. Sufficient unto the day are the troubles thereof.

His mind, in this respect, is at an opposite pole from Woodrow Wilson's. Wilson was a scholar. Roosevelt is an observer. Wilson disliked people and found it hard to get along with them. Roosevelt likes people and gets along with almost anybody. Wilson liked to be alone and often was. Roosevelt abhors to be alone and seldom is. Wilson's study was lined with books. Roosevelt's study is lined with ship models. Wilson read and got most of his ideas from reading. Roosevelt talks and gets most of his ideas from conversation. Wilson was a profound student of democracy but no democrat.

[5]

Roosevelt is not a profound student of democracy but he is a great democrat. Action incapacitated Wilson. Roosevelt thrives on it.

These differences do not add up to mean that Mr. Roosevelt is necessarily either intellectually superficial or lazy. But they do indicate that, however adequate his understanding may be, it is not a result of reflection. The President is not reflective. His mind works best when it has something concrete to work on and somebody concrete to work with.

Few Presidents have seen more people than Mr. Roosevelt does. Marvin McIntyre, whose business it is to keep down the number of Presidential appointments and to shoo out of the President's office when their time is up those who are lucky enough to get in, has as much trouble with the President himself as with the callers. The President's inclination is to see everybody. Once in his office, his inclination is to keep them there indefinitely. Mac hovers around, in front of the desk and behind the desk, holding the little sheet of paper on which the day's engagements are typed, inserting every now and then a "Mr. President" which Mr. Roosevelt understands and generally ignores, until the visitor catches on and makes the move to go. Mac has a soft spot in his heart for those who catch on early.

But this pleasure and ease in meeting people is more than geniality in the President. His callers are his source books. Almost everyone who has run the long gauntlet that leads to the Presidential office has something to contribute. Mr. Roosevelt, if it takes ten minutes or an hour, generally gets into the man's mind and comes out with the contribution. He hardly ever makes notes, either during a conversation or after it. Notes are not necessary. His mind sifts, tabulates and files and by the end of a long day of conversations the vast amount of information and ideas which have come out of other men's minds have been tucked securely away in Mr. Roosevelt's.

When, in his second term as governor of New York state, Mr. Roosevelt's Presidential prospects began to rise he turned deliberately to the business of informing himself on certain national problems with which, as a candidate, he would have to deal. He did not call for the most authoritative books. He called for the most authoritative people. They gave him what he wanted to know boiled down and separated from what he did not need to know and, therefore, did not care about.

This use of other people's minds is one, probably the chief, reason why, under Mr. Roosevelt, the rôle of Presidential adviser has assumed hitherto unequaled importance. Most of the members of the 1932 Brain Trust have long since found other fields of endeavor. But there will always be a Brain Trust as long as Mr. Roosevelt is President. The personnel shifts and changes. At present its chief members are Tom Corcoran and Ben Cohen. Six months hence Corcoran and Cohen may have moved on or out. But if they do, a new combination is sure to move in. A Brain Trust is indispensable to Mr. Roosevelt. Its members do his mental leg work. Unofficially they do much more than that. They see Mr. Roosevelt at those times when he is making up his mind what to do or say. They come loaded down with facts to help him in that process. They are, moreover, young men with ideas of their own. It is inevitable, therefore, that they not only put meat on his ideas, they exert an influence on the ideas themselves—more influence, often, than Representatives, Senators or Cabinet Members.

The President's mental operations not only require somebody definite to work with, they require—as I have said—something definite to work on. The problems he most enjoys are those which can be reduced to a diagram or a column of figures. In conversation about abstract ideas, Mr. Roosevelt's contribution is likely to be not an expansion of the idea but a concrete example that illustrates it.

This, I think, is a reflection of his Dutch ancestry—a very hard-headed, practical ancestry. The President has never had to work for a living. But he was never an extravagant son of the idle rich—partly, I suppose, because his family was not that rich. Nevertheless, there is a pronounced strain of practicality in him. He is money conscious and he likes account books. He is never quite so completely absorbed as when he sits down with

"The President!"

Danny Bell, Director of the Budget, gets out half a dozen well-sharpened pencils and some of his penny-a-pad scratch paper and figures out for himself how the government's income and outgo stand. Next to the Navy, the one Department in the government that is closest to his heart is the Treasury.

The struggle for economy and a balanced budget which is certain to characterize his second administration will be fought out between himself and his Congressional leaders. But back of that there will be another, more important struggle within himself between the frugal Dutchman who believes in balanced budgets and the New Deal statesman who has promised more than, inside a balanced budget, can be easily achieved. In such a struggle, the odds are on the Dutchman. In fact, I doubt if any of his reform legislation would give him as much satisfaction as the actual balancing of the budget.

In personal matters he is not penurious. But he is certainly not and never has been a free spender. Mrs. Roosevelt—startled one day to receive a long-distance telephone call from him—spoke of "my rather careful husband" and decided, immediately, that something extraordinarily important had happened. The President had called from Buenos Aires to tell her of the death of Gus Gennerich, his personal aide.

The President's first question about a project is likely to be "will it pay" or, even more likely, "how much will it pay?" He is reputed to be hostile to business.

But he has a great deal of pride in his own business transactions and I am inclined to believe that one of his unrealized ambitions is to be a successful business man.

When, therefore, the problem at hand is a concrete one the President masters it. I have seen him frequently, at press conferences, jump from one specific question about the government to the next with exactly the facts and information necessary to constitute the right answers. Occasionally—when he knows that the correspondents are likely to inquire about particularly intricate matters—he calls in experts. He generally forgets that they are there. At the first press conference after the reciprocal trade treaty was signed with Canada he had a small battalion of authorities back of his desk and a great pile of data on it. He never once referred to either. For an hour he leaned back in his chair and—although the treaty covered several hundred items of trade between the two countries—gave out from memory all the facts that the newspapers asked for.

This preference for and absorption with what is concrete and definite is highly useful in the ordinary business of running the government of the United States. But these have been more than ordinary times and Mr. Roosevelt has not been an ordinary President. He has done more than manage the business and run the government of the United States. He has put the government into a wholly new line of business. More important, even, than that he has changed the political buying habits of the nation. The result is that, today, the American people want and expect to get from Washington not only more of the things that they previously got, but a long list of new things. Thanks largely to Mr. Roosevelt's extraordinary salesmanship, the getting of those things, to the people who do not have them, has become one with the principles of Lexington and Concord and Independence Hall.

That may or may not be desirable. I am not concerned with that question at the moment. The point here is that —desirable or undesirable—the change is fundamental and its implications far-reaching. The problem involved cannot be reduced to figures or a diagram. But they are certain to be with us a long time after a good many more concrete issues have weathered away. Mr. Roosevelt, by his specific acts and his dynamic leadership, has created these consequences. It is still a question whether he understands and how much he has faced them.

My belief is that, in a general way, he understands them but that, so far as facing them is concerned he would say: "We will cross that bridge when we reach it." In other words, it will be time enough to meet the consequences when they have taken definite form and substance and have assumed proportions too large to be handled by anybody less than the President of the United States.

This procrastination is not only due to Mr. Roosevelt's dislike to consider problems which are still in the implication-stage. It is a result, also, of the fact that he has found that procrastination pays. Most of the troubles he is warned about never arrive. Why get ready for them, therefore, until they do?

The epidemic of sit-down strikes in the spring of 1937 is a good case in point. Every conceivable kind of pressure was exerted to persuade the President to make a declaration. Congressional leaders, some of them unaccustomed to speaking what is really on their minds in the Presidential presence, spoke out on this question and pounded the Presidential desk while doing it.

But the President was immovable. He knew, of course, how much ingenuity would be required to make a declaration that would please the worried Democratic spokesmen from the textile areas of the South and, at the same time, not displease John L. Lewis who was about to enter those areas. He refused to make the statement, not because he could not have mustered that much ingenuity, but because, bad as the sit-down situation seemed to be, he was willing to gamble on the chance that, if he waited, it would get better. Meanwhile, behind the scenes, he gave every possible encouragement to Governor Murphy to see to it that it did get better. And it did. For the moment, at least, the trouble blew over. Governor Murphy pulled out whatever administration irons were in the fire and prevented a good many more from getting near it. The President evaded the issue and the issue temporarily evaporated.

Meanwhile, he may or may not have made up his mind what he thinks about sit-downs. He may or may not have made up his mind what he thinks about the whole marching army of labor and of John L. Lewis who marches in its van. Mr. Roosevelt wrote the marching orders and, unofficially, gave John L. Lewis his out-in-front position. But it will be time enough to consider the issues involved when they turn up. Perhaps they never will.

In this, as on many other matters, including the sit-down strikers, the President's policy of delay is a gamble. Governor Murphy, for example, might have failed and the situation got out of hand too fast even for the President's intervention. But the President's gambling is backed by an uncanny intuition. He does not play bridge. But if he did he would bring the psychic bid to new levels of refinement. He reads the newspapers and listens to all sorts of advice. But in a tight spot he is apt to act on his hunches. He has found that it pays to play them. It would be incorrect to say that they serve as a substitute for intellectual effort. But they are certainly a very useful supplement to his understanding, particularly when he is dealing with issues which are somewhat unformed and indefinite.

His hunches, in turn, are backed by an almost equally uncanny knowledge of the state of the American mind at a particular time and on particular issues. He is generally right about what the American people will take

and when and how much they will take of it. There is
nothing in his experience to explain this understanding.
Dutchess County is no more typically American than
Surrey in Kent. His ancestral home at Hyde Park is
baronial in the best English tradition. Groton and Harvard and summers abroad are not the route to Main
Street. His travels in the United States have not been
knock-around trips, but usually as a candidate or as
President. Such traveling is about as good an introduction to the life and thought of the people of the nation
as a long-time residence in Washington, D. C.

Moreover, the men who have been closest to him are
not distinguished for their current familiarity with the
United States west of the Hudson River. Jim Farley,
for all his now somewhat over-emphasized rural boy-
hood and his frequent excursions into the hinterland,
will always be a New Yorker. Ray Moley, Rex Tugwell, Adolph Berle, Sam Rosenman, Tom Corcoran are
all Eastern, if not by birth, certainly by transplanting
and outlook.

Yet despite his own background and the provincialism
of his intimates, the President seldom goes wrong in his
forecast of popular reactions. He is sensitive to the public as some people are sensitive to the weather. There is
nothing general about it either. He can break down
public opinion section by section. No spokesman for the
Middle West, for example, can tell him much about the
psychology or the way in which, under certain condi-

tions, the inhabitants of the one-time Bible Belt will re-act. I have heard awestruck Congressmen, with ears flattened from having so long been kept so close to the ground, admit after a conversation with the President that he knew more than they did about the state of mind of their constituents.

The President, therefore, not only relies on his mind. He relies on his hunches and his intuitions. He has confidence not only in his ability but in his luck. When his mind plus his hunches and intuition all come out at the same point—and when they all seem to indicate that the time for action has arrived—then he turns on the steam, mental and physical, and does something about it. It has been remarked that—by waiting so long—he allows conditions to approach emergency proportions and then, not having given sufficient thought to what is in the making, he is obliged to improvise. But if he continues to improvise it is because he has been very lucky with his improvisations. The thing to do has very frequently turned up on his desk at about the same time that the necessity for doing it arrived there.

I think, moreover, that he has a peculiar zest for emergencies. He is inclined to look back upon the first few weeks of his first administration with special enthusiasm. Every day had its emergency and new ones sprouted every night. He slept little, ate less and set a pace that left his associates wan, hollow-eyed and groggy but left him clearheaded and invigorated. The success with which he handled that succession of crises is an indication of the quality of his mind when it is completely unlimbered and in action. If hunches and intuition help him to determine when the time for action has arrived, the need for action, particularly if it is pressing and the time definitely limited, stimulates his mind beyond its usual capacities.

It is because of these characteristics that Mr. Roosevelt, in all probability, has postponed either getting to the bottom of the ferment he has created or making any very specific plans to control and direct it. But the question naturally arises as to how, if his mental operations do not habitually deal in fundamentals, he has been able, none-the-less, to make fundamental alterations both in the point of view of the American people and in the objectives and processes of their government. The answer to that question is found, I think, not in his mind but in his emotions.

Someone once remarked that whether or not Mr. Roosevelt had a first-rate mind, there could be no doubt he had a first-rate set of emotions. That is true. He has a first-rate set of emotions, a set, moreover, which is amazingly expressive of the temper and the spirit of the times. He has never been one of the under-dogs. But he has always been on the side of the under-dog. A good many people still hold to the idea that his economic liberalism was evidence of his political shrewdness and not an expression of his own convictions. I think some of these people expect him, sooner or later, to drop his advocacy of reform, dissociate himself from the cause of the under-privileged and take his stand with "his own kind" among the Bourbons of the Knickerbocker Club—to which, by the way, he still pays dues.

He may let up on reform. But if he does it will not be because he is on the way back to the Knickerbocker Club. It will be because the reforms he lets up on cost money and will indicate that the hard-headedness of the Dutchman proved more potent than the emotions of the New Dealer. He will still be for the under-dog even though he is not engaged in any expensive undertakings in his behalf. That characteristic is too much and has been too long a part of him to be so easily got rid of. Strangely enough, his sympathies, like his hard-headedness, have their roots in his ancestry.

The President is proud of his forbears. He talks about them—interestingly and at length—whenever the opportunity offers, and particularly when he is at Hyde Park where some of the more notable among them look down from the walls. But he is especially proud of the fact that so many of his immediate ancestors were political nonconformists. His own father was a Lincoln Democrat. To have been a Democrat at all among the rich landowners of the Hudson Valley required a good deal of courage. To have been a Lincoln Democrat in 1863 was reckoned even worse than to have been a New Deal Republican in 1936.

ROOSEVELT—*And Then?*

But Franklin D. Roosevelt seems to get a boyish pleasure out of being a bit perverse and to enjoy doing what it is least expected that he will do. He, therefore, relished the fact that he was a Democrat if for no other reason than that almost all Hyde Park was Republican and inclined to be snooty about it. At any rate, when he went to Albany as a youthful member of the state Senate he had a nonconformist precedent to maintain. He maintained it with great enthusiasm. He jumped into the middle of the fight against the traction interests, the major fight of the day. At the outset his enthusiasm may have been stimulated by his knowledge of the shock he was giving the Hyde Park neighbors. But his wife was likewise enthusiastic about these good and slightly radical causes and she was tremendously serious about them. It was no lark with her, but a crusade. While her husband was in the midst of the traction fight in Albany, Mrs. Roosevelt, as energetic then as now, was making the rounds of New York City's tenements with Frances Perkins, then an amateur social worker, getting first hand knowledge of how the other half lived and passing on both her information and her zeal to her huband. She gave substance to his inclinations. She spurred a faith that might have flagged. In the end, the plight of the dispossessed became a crusade with him as it was with her.

When, therefore, the times turned ripe for that kind of gospel, he had the gospel ready for the times. The forgotten man had had his attention for a good many years before it got to the attention and caught the imagination of the country. His emotions, in 1932, were a mirror of the emotions of the American people. The things he had been trying to do for a long time in New York state were the things that they desired to have done for the nation. Mr. Roosevelt did not find out what the people wanted and offer it to them. He offered them what he had always maintained they ought to have and that, as it turned out, was what they wanted.

It would be a mistake to conclude that this sponsorship of the cause of America's depressed classes is entirely emotional. His sympathies fit into an intellectual pattern which undoubtedly has deepened since 1932 until to-day it constitutes his social and economic philosophy. He hardly ever expresses it. But here and there in his speeches and, even more infrequently, in conversation he indicates that it is there. In this, as in other matters, he has not reached his conclusions from reading but rather from his contacts. It is probable that the two men who helped him most to sharpen his thinking and give it definite outline in this regard were Adolph Berle and Rexford Guy Tugwell. Both of them were members of the 1932 Brain Trust. They shared Mr. Roosevelt's social enthusiasm. They had come to their conclusions by dint of wide reading, and hard thinking. Their operations had been almost entirely in the intellectual realm. But in that realm they had a plausible, definite, and, in general, a sound knowledge of what it was all about. Although much younger men than Mr. Roosevelt they were able to add something to the maturity of his thought. They did not change his opinions. But they helped to strengthen the intellectual foundations under them.

Just what it is Mr. Roosevelt believes and what he occasionally reveals he is driving at can be briefly summarized. His liberalism, for all his sympathy for the under-dog, is essentially hard-headed. He believes that liberalism is the best kind of hard-headedness. He believes in capitalism and the private profit system and shares the distaste of the best of the conservatives for radicalism and radicals. His definition of radicalism, however, is not that of the reactionary who looks upon all change as radical. He believes that change, far from being radical, is the essence of sound conservatism. If he were to grade the various existing dangers to the permanence of our institutions, I think he would put at the top of the list, not the radicals who advocate the destruction of those institutions, but the conservatives who oppose all changes in them.

Mr. Roosevelt has been frequently accused of hostility toward Big Business. I think he has such a hostility not because he is against bigness, in itself, but because he is convinced that many big enterprises and perhaps most big fortunes reached their size by practices which, however honest and legal, perpetuate conditions which are unhealthy for the system and a threat to its future. The story is told of a meeting of steel executives, in the President's office, to discuss an N.R.A. code for their industry. The representative of the Bethlehem Steel Company, upon leaving, told the President that Eugene Grace, President of the Company, had asked that his respects be paid to Mr. Roosevelt. Whereupon the President replied: "Pay my respects to Gene and tell him that he will never make a million dollars a year again."

The President's attitude toward Big Business men has the same convictions back of it as his attitude toward Big Business. I do not think he is against Big Business Men. But he is against dumbness. He believes that a considerable number of Big Business Men—he would probably single out the leaders of the United States Chamber of Commerce and the National Association of Manufacturers as examples—are, to put it baldly, dumb. He believes that if our economic system cracks up and they lose their financial skins, they will have only themselves to blame. Now, for a period the length of which no one can foretell, the massing forces at the other end of the economic scale are in a mood to settle with a compromise. That mood—if compromises are not forthcoming—will certainly not last. When it passes the consequences are likely to be disruptive and the very men who now stand adamant against the New Deal's half-way measures will probably stampede to Washington again as they did in the spring of 1933 pleading to be saved from the results of their own failure to accept those measures and make them work.

Mr. Roosevelt has always been for labor. But it is not my impression that, fundamentally, he has any greater fondness for the average labor leader, John L. Lewis in particular, than he has for the average industrialist. He probably would say, however, that the average labor leader is several degrees smarter than the average industrialist. And he does prefer smart people.

He is not for labor because he is against capital. He is for labor because he is for capital. What he has done to meet the demands of labor has been a result of the conviction that the concessions necessary to meet those demands are an investment in the safety of our institutions, just as the unwillingness of certain types of business leaders to concede anything is a threat to that safety.

His confidence in democracy, like that in capitalism, is genuine. He brought back from his South American journey the conviction that this western world represents the long-time strength and hope of democracy and that it was not too soon for the nations of these hemispheres to join together for its common defense. That idea is back of his big navy program. The responsibility of the democracy of the United States, as he sees it, includes a certain responsibility for all of the democracies of the new world.

He is undoubtedly conscious, sometimes acutely so,

of the fact that the ways of democracy are often ponderous and slow and that dictatorships—in the matter of short-cuts and quick action—have their pronounced advantages. But he looks upon the developments in the United States since 1932 as proof of the fact that even the most critical and pressing problems can be worked out inside the structures both of capitalism and democracy. To give sound and solid proof of that will not only strengthen democracy and capitalism in the United States but have a heartening effect upon the faltering defenders of those institutions elsewhere and a salutary effect upon their enemies. Such proof, I think he would agree, is the most significant achievement that his administration could produce.

It should be pointed out, however, that this faith has never had to survive a major defeat. The democracy that he believes in has always been, up to the present, a democracy that believes in him. The democratic processes have worked for, not against him. It is hard to say how his confidence in the judgment of the people would be affected if their democratic mandate rejected rather than endorsed him.

This is particularly a matter of speculation in his case because of the fact that his self-confidence is something more than that of a man who has reached the heights. Mr. Roosevelt is no mystic. But there is an almost mystical quality about his self-confidence, his destiny and the more than ordinary rightness of what he undertakes to do. He would not subscribe to the doctrine that the President can do no wrong. But his belief in himself has something of that doctrine in it.

That is another reason why he will probably delay consideration of the consequences of the New Deal until they are upon him. He is too sure of the end—not only in the rightness of what he is doing but in the certainty that he will get it done. The stars have taken counsel together and written it. He can afford, therefore, to refuse to be alarmed and to continue to shun the alarmists.

Moreover, this self-confidence will help to explain why, as the consequences of the New Deal develop through his second four years—the third-term temptation will become continually more pressing. It would be hard, at best, to choose from among his aspiring associates a man to wear his mantle. If, however, the Roosevelt program and, with it, the Roosevelt place in history are put in jeopardy by division and revolt then such a choice will be infinitely more difficult.

For more than four years now the slogan has been repeated, in the White House executive offices as elsewhere, that "there is only one Roosevelt." With due reference to the prospective contenders it appears to be obvious that there will be only one Roosevelt in 1940. He has not prepared a successor and I do not believe that he is now preparing one. More because of his personality than by deliberate intent he has not shared the spotlight with anyone else—not, at least, for long. He has been a one-man show. What he started will be far from finished at the end of eight years. The issue before him, therefore, is between a precedent which, however hallowed, is nothing more than a precedent and certain momentous undertakings which, in other hands than those that launched them, might well lose their significance and which, if there is any popular wavering, would appear unlikely ever to reach completion save by four more years of the power and magic of his leadership.

Mr. Roosevelt may never act on any such assumption. But the fact of his unshaken and unshakable faith in himself—his almost mystical self-confidence—makes it necessary to include such action among the possibilities. His decision is likely to be determined by his appraisal of the developing aftermath of the New Deal. I said at the outset that he has created an atmosphere, released forces and set a trend in the United States which are as much more significant than the New Deal as they threaten to be beyond its control. It is that Mr. Roosevelt, sooner or later, will make some effort to control them. If by 1940, they are not controlled then, lacking four more years in which to continue the attempt, he will face the unpleasant prospect of going out of office with the future of his objectives and his own destiny shadowed with uncertainty. Mr. Roosevelt would relish that prospect less than most men. I do not believe that there is anything Messianic in his belief in himself. But I am very sure that he would no more put his mission in jeopardy by surrendering it, too soon, to other hands than he would willingly consent to go down in history as a John the Baptist for some greater leader.

CHAPTER II

"THE WHITE HOUSE IS CALLING"

PRESIDENT ROOSEVELT has a great many intimates, few close friends and no cronies. He does not have cronies because, with all his sure-fire and sometimes hilarious geniality, he is not "chummy." His gregariousness is due to the fact that he wants diversion, entertainment or help, not because he wants companionship. Most of his close friends date from Harvard and Hyde Park and figure largely as pleasant recollections. But his intimates are probably more numerous than those of any President before him, their influence is greater and the speed of their turnover more rapid.

His intimates serve a good many useful purposes. They are foils for his mind and a stimulus to it. Some of them run his confidential errands and some of them help him to write his speeches. But all of them have this in common: they see him at those informal interludes in the Presidential day when the bars are down, no one is on parade, frankness is possible and, most im-

portant, ideas are readily sold. It is not the men who
see the President during working hours but those who
see him afterward who are the clew to what is on his
mind. The vigilant corps of newspaper men who keep
their eagle eyes on the front door of the White House
offices would do well to post at least one watchman at
the basement entrance. The men who slip in there and
up the backstairs to the private office of Marguerite Le-
Hand, which adjoins that of the President, are frequently bigger news than the reputedly bigger men for
whom the correspondents, in the upper lobby, keep
their pencils sharpened.

In fact, amazing as it is to observe how much the
Washington correspondents see, it is sometimes amazing
how much they miss. It is reliably reported that the
Presidential counsellor, for example, who saw Mr.
Roosevelt oftener than anyone else during the recent
campaign, had, perhaps, more influence on him than
any other person and, on at least three occasions, lived
for an entire week at the White House and only once had
his comings and goings recorded in the press. On that
one occasion, since he was a guest on the President's
yacht, obscurity was unavoidable. On other occasions so
the story goes he kept out of sight by a very simple
routine. He merely arrived at the White House before
the correspondents went on beat in the morning, stayed
indoors during the day or took his infrequent strolls
along the covered walk that runs from the President's

office past the swimming pool to the lower floor of the Mansion and left, when the time came to leave, by an unfrequented side door. This successful anonymity explains, in part at least, why he has outlived several generations of the President's less obscure intimates and advisers.

The President, of course, does not expect anonymity from his secretariat. From them he expects caution and, on most occasions, gets it. Marvin McIntyre, who handles the appointments and shakes the hands that do not get to Mr. Roosevelt, is known to be inclined to the company of the embarrassingly rich. But the aftermath of one incipient scandal in which "Mac" was caught at a utility lobbyist's cocktail party has had a restraining effect upon him. Mac's sin, in that case, was not so much in his choice as in his timing. The utility holding company fight was right at full tilt. On any ordinary occasion utility cocktails would have been as acceptable as any others. Mac had simply neglected to look at the legislative calendar. The President, in his relations with his secretaries, or for that matter with his own family, is no proctor.

Both Marvin McIntyre and Steve Early, whose job is the press, see the President constantly. But on matters of state it can hardly be said that their contact with him is influential. Mac tries to put an oar in now and then, usually with indifferent results. Steve seldom tries, unless in some way or other the press is involved. Then he is likely to jump in all over with a show of emotion which, in someone other than a conscious Southerner, would be called a "frenzy." But Steve cools down as rapidly as he heats up and I think the veteran newspaper men at the White House generally agree that, with him, they have had more forthright and squarer treatment than in several Presidential moons.

Mac, in many respects, has the more important post. He is the neck of the bottle leading to the President. The only people who get around him belong to that inside and unofficial family who know both Miss LeHand and the President well enough to make the approach through her. It is inevitable, since Mac is obliged to keep a great many important people from seeing the President, that a great many important people should dislike him thoroughly. And a great many such people do.

If there is anything on which a considerable number of this disgruntled host agree, it seems to be that Mac lets his personal feelings or his acquired patricianism play too large a part in his determination of those whom he marks for passage and those whom he bottles up. Whether or not the charge is justified, I am very sure that no Presidential secretary ever had a greater loyalty to his chief than Mac or troubled his mind less about what his chief was driving at. In so far as he understands, he probably disapproves. Anywhere else than in the White House with Mr. Roosevelt, Mac, up to the limit of his financial and social capacity, would be a Bourbon.

It is not likely, either, that Jimmy Roosevelt is much of an asset to his father on matters of public policy. Washington observers are still somewhat undecided as to whether in his present post he is an asset at all. No one denies that he has his father's looks and graciousness or that—when he speaks—his voice and manner of delivery are, either by chance or effort, almost exactly like those of the President. In fact, seeing young Jimmy Roosevelt turned out with so complete a set of his father's mannerisms brings not altogether favorably to mind the memory of another son of another Roosevelt who similarly modeled himself without too great success.

There is no doubt that Jimmy takes his job seriously. Whereas Steve Early seldom goes out socially and Marvin McIntyre's social circles are not notably New Deal, Jimmy gets around among the administration's intelligentsia. He undoubtedly brings back a good deal of interesting and useful information.

His more or less official assignment, of course, is Capitol Hill. Almost every one on Capitol Hill agrees, I think, that that assignment was a mistake. I do not mean that Jimmy has made any egregious blunders. Charlie West—the other official White House emissary at the Capitol—hovered solicitously over Jimmy's first ventures with Congress and kept him clear of the soft spots. But there has been nothing Charlie West could do about the fact that the young man is his father's son and it is that fact which Capitol Hill has resented in Jimmy as a White House lobbyist.

This resentment, doubtless, was inevitable. The average Senator or Representative, who may be in need of some word from the White House, feels that to send it by one of the President's own family puts the members of Congress at a disadvantage. This feeling has not been eased any by Jimmy's reported practice of referring to Mr. Roosevelt, not as the President, but as "father." When Jimmy says "father wants this" or "father is against that" he is generally taken at his word. But the Democratic members of Congress do not like it. Moreover, the father and son emphasis had unpleasant connotations. Jimmy may be the heir apparent at the White House. But at the Capitol the opinion seems to be that if he is the less that is said about it—for the next ten years—the better. No one will deny that he has come to the right place for his political apprenticeship. But the agreement is general that the more he takes his lessons in obscurity the more likely he will be to profit by them later on.

In the White House secretariat, but also distinct from it, is Miss Marguerite LeHand. "Missy," officially, is the President's personal secretary. She is the one indispensable member of the secretarial entourage. She not only understands what the President is driving at—and approves of it—she understands the President.

No one else breaks in on him with so little hesitation or knows so well when breaking in would not be judicious. No one talks up to him so frankly or understands when, in being in what she calls one of his "executive moods," talking up to him is not advisable.

It is difficult to reduce Miss LeHand's responsibilities to a single classification. Because she lives at the White House she is in on many of the President's most important conferences and is a party to almost all of his important decisions. Her disapproval of a person or a course of action is more difficult to overcome than that of anyone else save, only, Mrs. Roosevelt. Her approval is almost the next best thing to a Presidential O.K. Miss LeHand, I think, has very little to say as to what—in matters of state—the President ought to do. She does not lay any claim to economic learning or for that matter, and despite her fifteen years' association with the President, to any particular political shrewdness. But, whatever the President decides to do, Missy has a good deal to say as to the way in which he does it. Both in regard to individuals and in the President's relations with the public she has an uncanny sense of what is fitting and of what "just can't be done." Her arguments are not emotional. But she persists. And since the death of Louis Howe no other person close to the President is so frequently right.

Beyond all this, however, Missy's understanding of Mr. Roosevelt and her deft handling of him and of the people with whom he is surrounded are the chief reasons why the business mechanism of the White House runs with a minimum of friction and the President gets through day after day of strain with a minimum of avoidable irritation.

In the main, however, the White House secretariat is devoted and moderately efficient but not particularly influential on matters of public policy. A good many not too well-concealed hints have been dropped to the effect that the President would profit by a change. For some time there has been an undercover drive to "get Mac out." But the likelihood that he can be ousted is very small. Except for the death of Louis Howe and the appointment of James Roosevelt, there have been no changes in the secretariat since Mr. Roosevelt came to the White House. If any changes come now they are not likely to be by any suggestion from the President. Even if Mr. Roosevelt desired to make such a move, the fact that the pressure has been put on would probably prevent it. So far as his official personnel is concerned the President is not only unresponsive to pressure, pressure puts his back up.

Moving on the fringes of the secretariat, a political messenger and masseur, is Charles West, former Democratic Representative from Ohio, and, at present, Undersecretary of the Interior, a post he holds but does not fill. When Congress is in session Charlie West with Steve and Mac generally meet Mr. Roosevelt every morning

at the post-breakfast conference in the President's bed-
room. His little white cards, which he holds together
with a wide rubber band and carries in his vest pocket,
have a wide variety of odds and ends scribbled on them.
But they are all political. It is his business to listen to
Capitol Hill's complaints, give ear to its requests, carry
its current words of wisdom to the President and, in due
course, bring back the President's reply.

He does his often thankless job with unfailing good
humor. In fact, his unfailing good humor is probably
one of his liabilities. Charlie is a product of an evangelical tradition, he attended a small, denominational college in Ohio, he once served as a Y.M.C.A. secretary.
As a result, he narrowly escaped being sanctimonious.
Instead he has become what I suppose is Washington's
leading example of sweetness and light. His friendliness
is indiscriminate and his smile never diminishes. If he
says "no"—which he tries not to do—it is with an
affirmative emphasis.

In the first two years of the New Deal, Charlie was
one of the most vigorous and effective of the President's
spokesmen on the floor of the House. He gave up that
post to run for the Democratic nomination for the Senate in Ohio as an administration candidate against the
lukewarm and, as it turned out, unbeatable Vic Dona-
hey. His present post was a reward for that sacrifice.
He has undoubtedly been useful to the President. If he
has not been able to keep Congress in a continually

happy frame of mind, it is safe to say that its discontent has not been fed by any indiscretions on his part.

His reports to Mr. Roosevelt on the state of the Congressional mind are undoubtedly important. But his influence on the President's policies is negligible. On important matters, he does what he is told to do and seldom attempts to point out what ought to be done. I have never heard anyone in Washington say: "This is Charlie West's opinion." He, almost alone among the men who can be rated as advisers to the President, makes it a point not to have opinions or, at least, to keep whatever opinions he has to himself. He is a New Dealer, but without any private intellectual ax to grind. If he rolls up his sleeves it is to help Mr. Roosevelt and not to make America over.

The most seasoned and, strangely enough, the least battle-scarred of the men who have a major part in making up the President's mind is Samuel N. Rosenman, a justice of the Supreme Court of the State of New York. Judge Rosenman—"Sammy the Rose" in White House parlance—was the legal aid to Mr. Roosevelt when he was governor of New York. He got together the first Brain Trust in 1932. When, after the inauguration, the Brain Trust moved to Washington, Judge Rosenman stayed on in New York. That is one of a number of reasons why now—with his one-time associates scattered to the four political winds—Sam continues to come and go as much in the President's confidence as ever.

Sam has successfully kept himself not only out of the limelight, but well back in the shadows. When other, less shrewd advisers stepped forth after Mr. Roosevelt's first election, Sam stepped back. So far as I know none of the countless published photographs of the 1932 Brain Trust ever included Sam's picture. And yet he not only originated the plan for such a group, but he passed on the qualifications of those who applied for inclusion in it. During the campaign of 1932 headquarters were established in New York at the Roosevelt Hotel— close, but not too close—to those of the Democratic National Committee at the Biltmore. No one got past the door or, if they did, stayed long inside without the approval of Sam. He, alone among the group, knew the candidate, what he wanted and the kind of personalities he would welcome in his intimate circle. A number of other people have taken credit for the organization and effectiveness of the first Brain Trust. The President, however, gives the credit to Sam.

Another fact which helps to explain Judge Rosenman's longevity among Mr. Roosevelt's advisers is his unwillingness to call unless called for or to speak up unless spoken to. He, like Charlie West, has nothing to prove and no plan to put across. He is not committed to the evangelization of the world in this generation— unless Mr. Roosevelt is committed to it. In that case, and only if he is asked, he will go along with enthusiasm. But until he gets word that he is wanted he keeps well out from under foot. That is undoubtedly one reason why the President wants him so frequently.

Sam is a Manhattan American and, therefore, provincial. Most of what he knows about the country north of the Harlem River and west of the Hudson he has learned as a result of his association with Mr. Roosevelt. He never hurries and anyone who does hurry flusters him. He has, I should say, a more authentic sense of humor than any other of the President's close associates. He has a great respect for the office of President. But he is in no awe of Mr. Roosevelt. More, however, than anyone else, save Miss LeHand, he knows how to adjust his strategy to the President's moods.

In any economic classification of the President's advisers, Judge Rosenman would be rated as a liberal and not, in any sense, a radical. In fact, like some others, the Judge has probably gone farther left with Mr. Roosevelt than his own convictions and much farther than he would be willing to go with any other leader. He is not an economist or an historian even in the amateur sense. His value to the President—aside from his highly approved passion for anonymity—is due to his abundant supply of stable common sense, his ability to take an obscure document and, with a pencil and a few hours of solitude, inject some clarity into it and to the fact that he can be neither hurried nor alarmed.

Of the other members of the first Brain Trust—
Moley, after a campaign effort to revive his wilted
enthusiasm for the New Deal has left it altogether.
Tugwell, who parted amicably with the President, had
ceased to be an adviser long before the parting. Adolph
Berle, the most brilliant of the lot, still drops in, occasionally, on the President—whom he calls by the half-
affectionate, half-admonishing name of "Caesar." But
Fiorella LaGuardia, the Mayor of New York, has sup-
planted his political first love. Hugh Johnson, who was
an off-and-on Brain Truster is still off and on. Charlie
Taussig, who wormed his way into the aggregation, is
now, as President of the American Molasses Company,
the immediate boss of Rex Tugwell, and, having won
the favor of Mrs. Roosevelt, occasionally and generally
after much effort sees the President.

Of the members of the Cabinet, I believe that only
Henry Morgenthau, the Secretary of the Treasury, is
on terms of accepted intimacy with the President. Henry
Wallace, I think, is a little too serious and Cordell Hull
is much too serious. Homer Cummings is good company
but he is not an intimate. Miss Perkins is Mrs. Roosevelt's protégée. "Uncle Dan" Roper is always amiable
but I do not believe he is often called on. Jim Farley is
close to the President on matters of politics but, on questions of state, he is not one of those who are asked to
help to make the policies and—unless his advice is requested—Jim never offers any.

Henry Morgenthau, however, pre-dates the Presidency. He is a Dutchess County neighbor of the Roosevelt family. He, like the President, enjoys the Dutchess County status of "country squire." His interest in farming is not that of an amateur, but of a business man. All of his interests—and particularly his policies at the Treasury—are those of a business man. He keeps his farm in the black. The fact that he has not been able to keep the Treasury in the black is due to circumstances beyond his control and not to any lack of distaste for red ink. In this respect, too, he is like the President who, despite the present state of the Federal budget, has the greatest possible respect for "paying propositions."

Mr. Morgenthau—"Henry the Morgue"—is the one member of the Cabinet who drops in informally at the White House residence or who sees much of the President in other than business hours. He is not exactly entertaining. His touch is not quite light enough for that. I do not believe, either, that his influence in the Presidential circle can be called considerable. He is no more a New Dealer than most of his Wall Street friends, and his Dutchess County neighbors. The President keeps an eye and a hand on the Treasury Department as on no other. And Mr. Morgenthau, however much he may dislike some of the things he is obliged to put his hand to, takes an almost naïve pleasure in his Cabinet status and in the financial destinies over which, if he does not actually preside, he serves as a very important proxy.

There are two other men who are close to the President, whose part in helping him to make up his mind is considerable and whose influence is inclined to be conservative. The first of these is Frank C. Walker, a wealthy Montana Democrat living now in New York. Frank Walker, before the 1932 pre-convention drive got under way, heard Mr. Roosevelt speak at a New York luncheon. After the luncheon he met the Governor. They hit it off immediately. Walker, before nightfall of that day, is said to have sent a $10,000 check to Jim Farley for campaign purposes. Ever since then he has been inside the charmed circle.

I should say that Frank Walker accepts the New Deals, first and second, with more genuine conviction and fewer reservations than any other substantial pro-Roosevelt business man. Joseph P. Kennedy—the present chairman of the Maritime Commission—is mercurial as to his convictions and a prima donna in his relationships. Jesse Jones, the veteran of the Reconstruction Finance Corporation, has been close to the limelight for so long that his economic conservatism is tempered by his blossoming ambition for the Presidency. Sidney Weinberg, of Goldman-Sachs, who raised more money for the last campaign than any other man, is hardly a New Dealer despite the fact that during the

[41]

campaign he kept his enthusiasm for Mr. Roosevelt alive in a most difficult environment.

Frank Walker, however, never wavers. If he has any doubts he keeps them strictly to himself. He was a member of the President's council of campaign advisers. When, and if, Jim Farley leaves the Cabinet he could probably have that post but probably would not take it. The advice he gives the President, when his advice is asked for, is to keep going but to go slow. Unfortunately, except on matters of political finance and occasional appointments, his advice is not frequently asked for.

The second of more or less conservative influences is Mr. Donald R. Richberg. Don Richberg, in the declining days of the N.R.A., fell heir to the Hugh Johnson tornado. For a time, as head of the National Economic Council—the New Deal coördinating body—he was frequently called "the assistant President," a designation which bothered him more than it did the President. Later he left the government service and returned to his Washington law practice. When Joe Davies, the present, but hopeful Ambassador to Russia, entered on his diplomatic career he looked around for a lawyer of standing to take a partnership in his own, highly successful firm. The story is told that he asked the President for nominations. The President is said to have named Donald Richberg. At any rate, he got the invitation and accepted it.

Richberg, among Presidential counselors, is no genius and no scintillator. But his judgment is probably sounder and his feet planted closer to reality than that of anyone who has a continuing place in Mr. Roosevelt's intimate circle. He knows the country and travels enough to keep his knowledge up to date. In the Presidential presence he does not push his own views and he is inclined to go along on some things that he probably has little liking for. He is no obstructionist. But he is one of the few brakes.

Richberg supported the President's Supreme Court proposal. I doubt if he had any great enthusiasm for it. An effort was made, at the time when the authors of the bill were seeking to get out from under, to pin the entire scheme on him. I happen to know that, however large a hand he may have had in helping with the President's two addresses on the subject, he never saw the actual proposal until it appeared in the newspapers. Richberg did have a plan whereby he believed the New Deal might be fitted into the Constitution. But that plan did not involve warping the Supreme Court to fit into the New Deal.

Richberg, like Frank Walker, makes no effort to maintain his status as a White House intimate. He does not make it a point to see the President every week. In fact, he seldom makes any effort to see him. He is often described in the press as the chief of Mr. Roosevelt's advisers. But his contacts are too infrequent to give him that status. That, again, is unfortunate. If he were less occupied with his own business and had a greater ambition to have a hand in running the government of the United States he probably could be the President's chief adviser. The President, I think, would profit by it if he were.

The rôle of chief adviser is undoubtedly held at present by Thomas Corcoran—"Tommy the Cork." It might be more accurate to say that it is held jointly by Tom and his even more anonymous associate Ben Cohen. The two of them constitute a shadowy, fantastic team entirely unique, I should say, in the annals of American government. No one would dare to predict how long they will last but while they last most informed observers will agree that they exercise more influence at the White House and, through the White House, are more of a fearsome force throughout the entire reaches of the government than any pair of statesmen in Washington, in the Cabinet, in Congress or anywhere else.

Both young men are lawyers. Tom is a counsel for the Reconstruction Finance Corporation. No one that I know of ever found him there. Ben is a counsel for the Department of the Interior. Because he frequently uses a desk, Ben is sometimes in his office. In general, however, these posts serve as a place in which to keep a secretary and from which to draw a salary. If the President's reorganization plan goes through and he is given his six passionately anonymous assistants both Tom and

Ben will probably move, officially, into the White House where, for some time now, they have maintained unofficial headquarters.

Neither man is married. In fact, Tom's point of view about marriage carries out the idea of the late Louis Howe who once said that a law should be passed that an American citizen, to be eligible for the office of the Presidency, must be both a bachelor and an orphan. Tom resents married men—particularly if he has to work with them. "Their interests," he says, "are divided."

Tom and Ben suffer from such division. Of the two Tom is the more entertaining and Ben the more dependable. If Ben were free to consult his own preferences—which, under Tom's unrelenting drive, he is not—he would probably jump at a chance to return to the quiet life of a bona fide government lawyer or get out of the government entirely. He has an extraordinarily good legal mind. If, unlike Tom, he does not boast of any legal offers with "a six figure salary," it is not because he would find it difficult to get a good job.

His ambition, I think, is to use his legal ability in the business of the law, undisturbed by the boisterousness and the risks of politics or the nocturnal brainstorms of his partner and roommate. He belongs to the New Deal left wing. But he is not a Frankfurter product. His law school was the University of Chicago. His radicalism, therefore, is less evangelical than Tom's. Left alone, Ben could probably circulate, unsuspected and with a free conscience, among the members of the Chevy Chase Club or enter a New York legal firm and find a considerable measure of satisfaction in the company of his conservative associates at the bar.

But it is not likely, so long as Tom chooses to make Washington his Happy Hunting Ground, that Ben will be left alone. Tom is the salesman and Ben handles the production end of the business. Tom has ideas and Ben puts meat on them. Tom says a thing can be done and— if it is the sort of thing that has to be intelligibly reduced to paper—Ben does it. Tom would be scintillating without Ben. But he would be much less useful.

Tom served a spell in Wall Street and is said to have been burned. He first came to Washington as a secretary to the late Justice Oliver Wendell Holmes. He has Holmes' sayings at the tip of his tongue for almost every occasion. His first government job was in the Reconstruction Finance Corporation in the Hoover administration. His road to eminence in the New Deal was opened for him by Felix Frankfurter. Tom is a graduate of the Harvard Law School and, while there, Frankfurter put his cross on him as he did on Jim Landis and a number of other subsequently important New Dealers. Unlike Landis—whose radicalism has been tempered by his successful effort to make the Securities Exchange Commission a judicial rather than a punitive body and whose status, among the Frankfurter liberals, has thereby been impaired—Corcoran has never departed from the Frankfurter pattern. He has probably improved on it.

It is impossible to know how much Frankfurter pulls the strings by which Tom dances. Certainly the two are very close. Tom, whose devotion to the technique of telephone conferences has become a Washington tradition, is said to have frequent, long-distance consultations with his Harvard patron. Frankfurter, himself, seldom shows up in Washington.

When, in the spring of 1933, the crusade was just getting under way and reforms were sprouting at every Washington lunch-table, Tom and Ben undertook the preparation of the Securities Exchange Act. It is generally conceded that—unlike some of their subsequent efforts—they did a good job. Since then, they have had a hand in the preparation of many of the important New Deal measures, particularly those which have had to do with the regulation of business. It was as a natural result of this important activity that they finally made a place for themselves at the Presidential council-table. As a matter of fact, although both men made the place only Tom occupies it. Ben seldom puts in an appearance at the White House.

Tom undoubtedly has what it takes. For one thing, he is one of the most entertaining people in Washington. He is a talented pianist and an even more talented accordionist. In fact, Tom's accordion is one of his major political assets. Its always acceptable use has frequently broken the ice and prepared the way for him in situations where even his wit and wisdom might have failed. He sings while he plays and his repertory of Irish folk songs and sea chanties is almost inexhaustible. In every sense of the word, therefore, Tom is a social asset. The fact that he has not become one of the lions of Washington society is not due to any lack of interest on the part of Washington. Tom is too single-minded to waste his time and too wary to run the risks.

That quality of single-mindedness is another of his major assets. In all his waking hours—and his sleeping hours are few—Tom moves with well-organized concentration. He believes in a planned economy and he practices it on himself. I once met him at a tea dance given by an official too high in the government to be ignored. He came in late, shook hands with the host and hostess, nodded to a few people, whispered in my ear, "This doesn't fit into my scheme" and disappeared.

Moreover, he knows the government as few people in it. For four years he has been building up a miniature staff of subordinates which is ceasing to be miniature. The staff consists of able young men whom he has recruited from private life, indoctrinated with his ideas and planted, strategically, through the various government departments and administrative agencies. They are said to report to him frequently on a variety of things giving him an inside track not only to the facts about the various activities of the administration, but also to the gossip about the various administrators. He is the best single source of information in Washington.

Tom is probably a considerable distance to the left of the New Deal. When the setting makes it judicious, he is evangelical about it. I do not know, however, how long Tom would remain as far to the left as he seems to be if the prevailing winds took a turn. There is certainly no sign of chronic radicalism in the enthusiasm and the frequency with which he refers to his possible "six-figure" salary. I think it is more likely that the force which maintains Tom's drive is not that of deep-seated conviction but, rather, the love of power.

Tom once remarked to me that the great men of history were those who "fished in troubled waters." Those, unquestionably, are the kind of waters in which Tom is fishing. The opinion on Capitol Hill seems to be that he has even had something to do with troubling them. It may be that the criticism which his Supreme Court lobbying aroused will impair his status. His subsequent emergence as the "goat" for all the anti-administration columnists and special writers has destroyed his anonymity and may curtail his usefulness. But in his case, as in that of other New Dealers whose heads have been demanded, the President is likely to resent the pressure. He undoubtedly recognizes—and Tom, I think, is already reconciled to the fact—that to an administration which so bitterly antagonizes so many influential people,

a "whipping boy" is almost a necessity. Having served
in more unpleasant capacities, Tom will probably consent
to serve in this. On the other hand he may—as he often
has threatened to do—go back to private life and claim
the fortune that he apparently believes awaits him there.

I do not think that Mr. Roosevelt's long-time objectives are subject to much change by his counselors. But
his tactics are subject to a great deal of change. More,
I believe, than most Presidents, Mr. Roosevelt's immediate moods and inclinations are influenced by those
with whom he is in intimate, informal contact. And it
is largely from his moods and inclinations that his tactics
spring. At the time of his second inauguration, the President unquestionably was inclined to put on the brakes,
his mood was to go through with an Era of Good Feeling. That subsequently the Era of Good Feeling was
abandoned and the brakes taken off was largely due to
the fact that, at the time, he was chiefly surrounded by
a group of brakes-off advisers.

From a standpoint of the President's advisers, there
is this significant difference between the First and Second New Deals. The Moley-Tugwell-Berle combination which was most active at the White House at the
launching of the First New Deal did not cut the President off from conservative counselors. In fact, a review
of the first year of Mr. Roosevelt's first administration
would reveal that, day after day, a steady stream of
moderately conservative business men came and went at

the White House. Some of them came and went often enough to rate a quasi-advisory status. They may not have agreed with the President and the President may have not been able, at all points, to persuade them. But, at least, he was not cut off from conservative counsel.

The Second New Deal, however, was launched without the benefit of counsel. One of the most portentous facts about the first year of Mr. Roosevelt's second administration is that he has been almost entirely cut off from conservative counselors. The line which was drawn in 1933 and thereafter between reactionaries and moderate conservatives apparently is drawn no longer. Moderate conservatives, apparently, are no more welcome than reactionaries. It is not reactionary Big Business which has become persona non grata at the White House. It is Big Business. A blind spot has appeared which blankets the area in which a major part of the economic activity of the nation is carried on. It would be absurd to contend that that blind spot is a creation of the President's advisers. The inclination had to be there. But it is undoubtedly a fact that the President's Second New Deal advisers have been of a mind, not to curb the tendency, but to encourage it.

Meanwhile, Mr. Roosevelt's counselors are not by any means his cronies. Most of them, socially, would not even be called his close friends. Their survival is dependent upon a number of things: their ability to entertain, their cleverness to converse, the usefulness of their particular stock of knowledge, their enthusiasm to go the way the President is going, their facility to adjust themselves to his moods. By whatever qualities they keep his favor, the President's dependence upon them has lifted their status to a place more potent than that held by any of their kind—with the possible exception of Colonel House—in any previous administration. Not all of their telephone calls are prefaced by the magic formula: "The White House is Calling." But the White House mark is on them and their comings and goings, their yeas and nays are not those of ordinary men.

CHAPTER III

THE ROOSEVELT MOOD AND THE DEMOCRATIC TEMPER

MR. ROOSEVELT abhors prima donnas. His feeling in the matter is a result of his own experience. His entourage has had some—not too much—brilliance in it. It has almost always had too much temperament in it. That was particularly true during the early months of the first New Deal, when, to keep his intellectuals together and functioning, the President was obliged to spend some time out of almost every day smoothing the ruffled feathers of the young men who—without warning or apprenticeship—he had catapulted into places of importance. And some of the most easily ruffled feathers belonged, not to his young men, but to the members of his own Cabinet. In fact, one member of the Cabinet is said to have resigned so often that the process of persuading him to withdraw his resignation has become a part of the established White House routine.

Mr. Roosevelt, himself, is not temperamental—not, at least, in the ruffled-feather sense. He has what some of his close associates call "executive moods." On these occasions—usually induced by some irritating circumstance such as an unfavorable decision from a stiff-necked Supreme Court—his pleasantries are less spontaneous, he is less readily diverted from what is strictly business, he makes no parenthetical wise-cracks, himself, and does not respond to the wise-cracking of anybody else. In short, he is what—in most people—would be called exasperated.

That an "executive mood" seldom reaches the exasperation point is due, I think, to the fact that his geniality is chronic and his sense of humor too acute to be long repressed. There are not many points at which Mr. Roosevelt resembles Calvin Coolidge. But the temper which he shows to the world is, on the special Roosevelt level, almost Coolidgian in its evenness.

But if the President's feathers are not easily put out of place it is not for lack of temperament but because his temperament is more than skin deep. It operates well below the surface. It does not show up in small and superficial matters. It is neither easily aroused nor, conversely, easily suppressed. Like the temperament of Woodrow Wilson, however, it is ominous when it is aroused. And, again like Wilson's, it is backed by a long memory.

Mr. Roosevelt's philosophy accounts for what he is

trying to do. His temperament explains, in large part, the way in which he is trying to do it. Most of the good and the evil in his philosophy can be credited or debited against his mind. The good and the evil in his tactics will have to be chiefly charged against his temperament.

Since the 1936 election and particularly since the 1937 session of Congress, the conviction seems to have grown that the President's philosophy is sounder than his tactics. In his second inaugural address he referred to the change in the "moral climate" of America. He had in mind, I think, the increased sensitivity of the average citizen, and of his government, to the plight of the under-privileged and the dispossessed. That change has undoubtedly taken place. The Roosevelt philosophy has become the American philosophy. Or, rather, the Roosevelt leadership has revived a philosophy which had always been American and happened to be Mr. Roosevelt's. At any rate, except among the diminishing Die-Hards, Mr. Roosevelt—if he has not given the country a new philosophy—has at least led to a revival of faith in an old one. Most of his general aims have been put beyond dispute. The country—save for an occasional Tom Girdler—believes in them.

The remaining and unresolved issue concerns tactics. If the President's tactics derived from the same source as his philosophy the issue would be an insignificant one. But they do not derive from the same source. As I have indicated, they are less a product of his mind than of his temperament. His temperament, in some particulars, is characteristically American. But its implications, so far as they affect the way in which the American government does business, are not characteristically American. At some points they do not appear to be in the American tradition at all.

What these implications are can, I think, be best understood after a summary of what the philosophy is. Mr. Roosevelt's gospel—and that of the New Deal—has been preached for a long time in the United States and preached and more extensively practiced in a good many other countries. The fact that many of its most effective preachers have been Socialists does not—contrary to the best reactionary opinion—make it socialistic. The Socialists are also for world peace and a considerable number of other good things. Many of the New Dealers, and certainly Mr. Roosevelt, believe that it will be possible to work out this philosophy inside the structure of capitalism. But it is fairly clear that, to work it out to the end, however it leaves the private profit system, will leave the government of the United States much farther to the left than it is to-day. I think Mr. Roosevelt would say that—with a rising intelligence at the lower economic level—only a government farther to the left will be a safe government.

There are three major points in the Roosevelt philosophy. The first of these is the belief that the place to measure and insure the health of our economic system is at the bottom, not at the top of it. The United States, in the past, has widely practiced what might be called the drip system of economics. That is, in government and in industry we have gone on the assumption that if we could insure prosperity at the top, enough of it would drip through to the bottom to satisfy the legitimate demands of the people who were lodged there and provide them with as much happiness as could be granted without seriously cutting in on the profits of those at the top or seriously upsetting the protective belief that those at the bottom deserved to be there. That is what is generally behind the references one hears about economics as "natural law." If industry, finance, and government combined to look after the man at the top, natural law would provide for the man at the bottom.

Mr. Roosevelt's economic philosophy is at exactly the opposite pole. He does not believe that in such a filtering economy the process is automatic or that the amount filtered is adequate. In his opinion the only kind of capitalism that can survive, or deserves to, is one in which our traditional economic thinking has been changed and our traditional economic practices reversed until we have a system designed, first of all, to insure prosperity at the bottom on the assumption that, then, a fair share of that prosperity will bubble through to the top. He is against leaving our system to the mercy of the rugged individualists because he has observed that rugged individualism leaves too many of our people to the mercy of the elements.

If what he proposes curtails the benefits of our economic order for those at the top it is not because he wants to destroy the system but because he believes the only way to save it is to guarantee a larger cut-in for those at the bottom. He believes that this is not only sound justice but also sound economics. And he does not believe that this end can be achieved by the voluntary action of benevolent employers. Too large a minority is not benevolent enough.

It is my opinion that—with all his urge to balance the Federal budget—the President goes more than half-way with the La Follette conviction that the only way to get the country on a permanent and safely prosperous basis is to set out deliberately to raise the standard of living of America's under-privileged millions by Federal spending. In fact, his present policy on relief constitutes a half-way endorsement of that conviction. Senator La Follette maintains that the policy is relatively ineffective because it is only half-way. The President's inclinations are too frugal to allow him to go farther than that. Nevertheless, in the abstract he would probably agree that, from the point of view not only of justice but also of economic sense, a Federally subsidized boost to the standard of living, i.e., the purchasing power, of those at the bottom of the scale is sound doctrine.

The President's economic philosophy has a second, and corollary, conviction which has to do with what we have been inclined to regard as the paramount importance of property rights. I do not believe that the President looks upon the protection of property rights as an end in itself. He regards it, rather, as a means to an end. The end is the protection of personal rights and the betterment of people. Mr. Roosevelt would probably maintain that no other principle, passed down from our fathers, has been so distorted to serve ends that were vicious as this. Property rights have been—and among a happily diminishing group still are—the patriotic camouflage for a vast number of wholly unpatriotic practices.

That is why the President has never expressed any appreciable alarm over the accusation that his policies constitute an invasion of property rights and are, in consequence, the likely preface to a revolution. It seems to be his conviction that revolutions do not come as a result of carelessness about property rights; that they are far more apt to come as a result of carelessness about human rights. When the philosophy of property rights is expounded to the President I think his answer is something like this:

"All right, I'll whoop it up with the best of the conservatives about property rights if they will agree to whoop it up with me about human rights—about child labor and sharecroppers and decent wages and hours and housing. The trouble with the people who get excited about property rights is that those are usually the only rights they get excited about."

The third major conviction in the Roosevelt philosophy is one which serves to implement the first two. This is the belief that there is no area or activity in American life—political, economic, or social—which is necessarily beyond the concern and, if required, the intervention of the Federal government. If this does not mean that Mr. Roosevelt proposes an unlimited extension of Federal power, it does mean that he aims to have such an extension of power wherever, in any area or situation, the welfare of the American people is not being and, in his opinion, cannot readily be protected by any other authority—public or private.

Most of the legislative proposals in Mr. Roosevelt's first New Deal can be explained in the light of these three convictions. The N.R.A., in its long-run significance, was a government-sponsored effort—in areas where the government had not gone before and out of which the Supreme Court ejected it—to bring business and industry to abide by certain minimum standards of humanitarianism. Boiled down, the Triple A is an effort, backed by the United States Treasury, to establish and maintain prosperity among a class of our people whose depression began in 1921. The Social Security

Act, the Labor Relations Act, the Securities Exchange Acts, the Bank Deposit Insurance Act, the Tennessee Valley Authority, the Home Owners Loan Association, the Resettlement Administration, and a long list of other laws and agencies are aimed, primarily, to build a more substantial undergirding for those who are lowest in the economic scale and to provide for them a larger share in the nation's income. If some of these laws and agencies involve competition with private business or an unprecedented curtailment of the freedom of private enterprise, and if they require heavy taxes in the upper brackets, Mr. Roosevelt would probably say:

"Better moderate concessions now, while our low-income citizens are in a mood for moderation, than the kind of an upheaval which will come when 'the long, long patience of the plundered poor' has been exhausted."

Now Mr. Roosevelt's philosophy, in so far as it is accepted and becomes the basis for the normal economic procedures of our government, clearly constitutes a departure from what some people have been pleased to call the American tradition.

It certainly writes finis to the laissez-faire chapter of American history. The area in which rugged individualists can be rugged will never again be as large as it was and even in that area the ruggedness will be subject to a government scrutiny that may cramp its style. Although somewhat discredited as a slogan, a planned economy is still a chief corner stone of the Roosevelt program. Inside the plan men will continue to make money and lose it, to launch new enterprises and expand old ones, to succeed and fail and be regarded according to their efforts, their ingenuity and their luck. But boundaries will be fixed for the scope of their operations and rules established for the nature of their operations. The present senior partners in the system—having played a different game—may not like the new one. It is my guess that, given another ten years, the junior partners will not only be adjusted to the new game, they will heartily approve it.

This philosophy, likewise, puts an end, in most important particulars, to the hoary doctrine of states' rights. In his public declarations, Mr. Roosevelt—aware of what a hornet's nest has been built around this subject in the Democratic South—has walked with caution in its vicinity. But neither the feelings of the South nor the more recent and obvious embracement of this principle by many northern conservatives has served to alter his program. It is obviously Mr. Roosevelt's belief that almost all of what goes on in an individual state—if it is of economic significance—is a national problem. He appears to be just as clearly of the opinion that the social conscience of the Federal government is, in general, more sensitive than that of state governments; and that, if we are a nation, the welfare of the people in any particular geographical area is more important, nationally, than the preservation of the geographical sanctity of the area.

Expressed in terms of the alterations it involves in our system, it may be that the Roosevelt philosophy has not become, unqualifiedly, the national philosophy. But these alterations are not, specifically, what Mr. Roosevelt is trying to bring about. They are the consequences of what he is trying to bring about. Whatever the opinion may be on the consequences, I believe that the nation's moral climate has changed sufficiently to insure an overwhelming agreement on the objectives. Moreover, Mr. Roosevelt has brought about a sufficiently potent political articulation among those who stand to gain by these objectives to make it unlikely that any succeeding administration will dare to abandon or, for that matter, seriously to curtail them.

Mr. Roosevelt, in his personal relationships, is wholeheartedly a democrat. His democracy, in fact, is of the genuine and uninhibited sort which sometimes appears in high born people who have nothing to lose by friendliness and nothing to gain by patronizing. Snooty people are as much on his black list as prima donnas.

But that kind of democracy is not peculiar to democracies. Despots and dictators can be—and have been— that kind of a democrat. There is more to democracy than accessibility, friendliness, or even good will. It is more than a way in which any particular individual may do business. It is a way in which society may do business. And there is a qualitative difference between the two operations. Devotion to the practice of individual democracy does not necessarily involve a happy acceptance of the checks and balances, the curbs, the vetoes, and the compromises that the practice of political democracy always requires.

Moreover, democracy is more than a tool. It is not something that exists merely for the production of good things. For all believing democrats, it *is one* of the good things, the most important of them. Other forms of government, notably dictatorships, get some things done more expeditiously than democracies. Given a benevolent dictatorship, most of the so-called good things that democracies strive for could probably be achieved more expeditiously. Few people, I think, will defend democracies on the ground that they are either the quickest or the most efficient method by which a political society can do business.

The best defense of the democratic process is that the process, itself, has virtue, quite apart from any concrete thing which, at the particular moment, it may be achieving. That virtue springs from the fact that there is something to be gained when a people think and act for themselves which is over and above the specific and tangible things which their thinking and acting produce. A democratic government operates on the assumption that the state exists for man, not man for the state, and on the further assumption that there is no contribution by the state to man half so significant as that which makes both the speed and the nature of man's social progress dependent upon the growth and exercise of his own free mind and the expansion of his own independent spirit.

A democratic mechanism—as such—has little enough in its favor. It is unspectacular, lumbering, and inefficient. But a democratic people have a good many things in their favor. And those things, it seems to me, indicate that there is more of value in the mechanism than the sum total of what, concretely, it turns out. The mechanism may not turn out good roads, adequate housing, and decent working conditions as rapidly as we would like. But it is worth saving anyway. In fact, it is so much worth saving that it is a part of the very essence of the democratic faith to believe that it is better to get these things slowly—by the democratic process—than to get them more rapidly any other way.

If it is true that some special virtue inheres in the democratic process, it is also true that the successful use of that process requires, in individuals and in a nation, certain definite characteristics. Taken together these characteristics constitute what might be called the democratic temper. Individuals and nations possess the democratic temper in different degree and its exercise varies with the times and the situations. Nevertheless, a democracy depends, for its working success, upon the extent to which the democratic temper has taken hold of and become habitual among a people.

[65]

ROOSEVELT—*And Then?*

Mr. Roosevelt undoubtedly has a great faith in democracy. But I am sure that he appraises democratic institutions almost exclusively in terms of the needful things that they are getting done. I do not believe that the idea occurs to him that some needful things might better be done more slowly if doing them faster would weaken the democratic process. The idea probably has not occurred to him because, in certain significant particulars, his temper is not the democratic temper.

For one thing he is spectacular. Democracies have no lack of spectacular individuals in them who produce, in their particular fields of operation, spectacular results. But the democratic mechanism, itself, is not geared to spectacularism. Dictatorships can remake society by Five Year Plans and Four Year Plans. The democratic way is here a little and there a little. When there is government by edict it is possible to go a long way in a short time—or appear to. When the government is democratic that is not possible. Democracies move slowly because, in a democracy, so many things have to be taken into account before it is possible to move at all. In an emergency—a war or an economic catastrophe—democracies do speed up. But the resulting spectacularism is almost entirely in proportion to the degree to which democracy, itself, is suspended.

Mr. Roosevelt was obliged to be spectacular in the early days of his first administration. The emergency required it. And all the parties to our political system agreed to the virtual suspension of the democratic process that resulted. But in his second administration Mr. Roosevelt is no less spectacular than in his first. The Second New Deal calls for action as drastic and as rapid as the first. But in this case—and quite apart from the desirability of the stated objectives of the Second New Deal—no emergency exists.

Even then, Mr. Roosevelt may get his way. If he does get his way then we in the United States will have demonstrated—so that even dictatorships can understand—how much in how short a time a democracy can achieve. But it will also be perfectly plain—as certain observers in dictator-ruled countries have already pointed out—that our achievements will be in part at least a result of the degree to which the democratic process has been short-cut.

I do not believe that Mr. Roosevelt is spectacular merely for the sake of the spectacle. He is spectacular because he loves action—not skirmishes, but big action. I think he is sincerely devoted to peace. But if war were wholly unavoidable, I am sure that no admiral of the navy would take to it with greater enthusiasm. He relishes action on that scale. The economic emergency, in the first administration, was his war. Up to the present the emergency in his second administration has been largely synthetic. But he is none-the-less pushing ahead on a war basis.

That, again, is not characteristically democratic. Democracies, customarily, do not keep a people in a continual state of psychological mobilization. Dictatorships do that because—in a successful dictatorship—it is necessary to find some substitute for the free employment of the minds of the people. In a democracy people have to have time to catch their breath in order to take their bearings. In a dictatorship they are not given as much time as that, for fear they may take their bearings.

Patience is also unquestionably a part of the democratic temper. Like most men of action Mr. Roosevelt is impatient. Incidentally, the patience required in a democracy is an exceedingly active virtue. This is due to the very nature of that kind of government. It is presumably impossible, in a democratic government, to get any important thing done until a majority of the people, or their elected representatives, are persuaded that it ought to be done. The process of doing things that way is a slow process for those who are in a hurry. A very high and very active order of patience is required if one is to persuade a majority of the people and to persist through the long pull until they are persuaded.

This, it seems to me, involves not only patience with those who are slow to be persuaded but, also, with those who cannot be persuaded at all. That is what democrats mean by respect for the rights of minorities. The rights of minorities should, but do not always, include the opinions of minorities. It is quite probable, for example, that a good many of the Democrats who opposed the

President in the recent Supreme Court fight were honest. But the prevailing opinion in administration circles seemed to be that very few of them were honest. Whenever honesty is made synonymous with support for those in power, then democratic government will be on the way out.

Moreover, this patience which is a part of the democratic temper involves the willingness, not only to take the long and slow way around, but also to accept less than is asked for. It is only dictatorships which do not have to compromise. In democracies it is often healthier to compromise even when compromising is not necessary. There is some virtue in accepting a middle-of-the-road solution which an overwhelming majority of the people will approve instead of pressing for a more drastic solution which, even though it is adopted by a bare majority, will leave vast numbers of the people dissatisfied or uncertain. Whole loaves, won by a narrow margin, sometimes turn out to be less satisfying than half loaves which have a more substantial approval.

The Supreme Court issue illustrates this point. The President, relatively early in that fight, could have had a compromise which—in all essentials—would have included his original proposal and, at the same time, would have won the backing of an overwhelming majority of the United States Senate. Quite apart from any effect which the final solution of that problem may have upon the judiciary, it seems to me that Mr. Roosevelt, in rejecting a compromise when compromising was easily possible, missed an opportunity to demonstrate the conviction that the democratic process is more than what can be jammed through it. His advisers declared that he was "in no mood for compromise." That was unfortunate. It was unfortunate because, in a democracy, the mood to compromise is indispensable. It may turn out to have been unfortunate for Mr. Roosevelt because, this being a democracy, it is necessary to take respectful account of those who disagree.

But the chief long-time political significance of the Supreme Court issue lies in the fact that Mr. Roosevelt's plan was a short-cutting of the democratic process. Here was a question which clearly involved a basic alteration in the machinery by which the nation, in judicial matters, did business. The country had voted on the objectives which, by this alteration, were to be made constitutional. They had voted on the Roosevelt philosophy, and approved it. They had not voted on this particular Roosevelt tactic. They might have approved that, also, but it would have been by a narrower margin. The point is that they were not given a chance to vote.

Mr. Roosevelt's acute sense of immediacy, his impatience, his inclination to be stubborn—in short, his temperament—dictated another course. That course—whatever the measure of its immediate success—was not the democratic one.

The administration's arguments against submitting a

Constitutional Amendment to the people were presumed
to be arguments for the President's plan. In effect, however, they were arguments against the democratic process. It was the administration's contention that a Constitutional Amendment is too slowly ratified, that one
cannot be sure that it will ever be ratified at all, that
a concentrated opposition in a minority of states can
block any action. These things are unquestionably true.
But if, being true, they are unfortunate, then the fault
lies with the system and the arguments constitute attacks
upon it.

The basic question at issue was not whether the President would have his way, but whether he was willing to
run the risks involved in getting his way by the methods
that democracy prescribes. He did not choose to get his
way by these methods. Neither his failure to submit
a Constitutional Amendment nor the coercive tactics
used in the effort to force a bill through a reluctant
Congress were a credit to democracy or, for that matter,
in the democratic tradition at all.

And there is more involved in this than Mr. Roosevelt's temperament. His chief support for his Court
measure came from the more aggressive wing of organized labor. Organized labor is out to get certain—and
generally desirable—things for itself. Quite naturally,
it values the immediate getting of those things above
everything else. In the midst of its rapid drive for them
there is very little desire or opportunity to inquire, too

carefully, whether the tactics employed are democratic or otherwise. Organized labor does not feel itself—any more than organized business—to be the guardian of the democratic process. It is out to get what it can while the getting is good. The duty of the government, on the other hand, is to determine whether the getting methods are obnoxious or dangerous to our system, and to require some measure of conformity to traditional American practice. In this instance, however, it was the government which set the precedent for nonconformity.

Impatient labor leaders, like impatient business men and impatient politicians, undoubtedly feel that democracy is a slow way of achieving their objectives. In the Supreme Court issue the administration agreed that democracy was slow—in fact, that it was too slow. The administration did not seek to bring the impatience of labor within the moderating confines of the democratic system. On the contrary, it put the seal of official approval upon that impatience by, itself, going outside the system. If the administration had won, once, by a short-cut, it would have had much more difficulty, the next time, in persuading impatient groups who might be in power to take democracy's long way around. When, on basic questions, it becomes habitual to short-cut democracy, then we will have government, not by democracy, but by short-cuts.

It is for these reasons that the unresolved issue of the Second New Deal does not concern the President's philosophy and objectives so much as his temperament and his tactics. His philosophy and objectives concern economic changes which, as I have indicated, are generally acceptable to the people. His temper and his tactics concern political changes which are probably much less acceptable. And long after Mr. Roosevelt's temperament has ceased to be an active factor in the American scene, the precedent which those changes establish is likely to be a source of encouragement to men who are in too much of a hurry to be democratic.

CHAPTER IV

THE UNITED STATES CHANGES STREAMS

In 1932, the United States changed horses. By 1937, it was changing streams.

It was Mr. Roosevelt's aim to keep the democratic machinery of the government of the United States intact while he brought the country through the crisis that confronted it at his first inauguration. He succeeded. At his second inauguration all the wheels were where they were at his first. There were, even, some new wheels.

In view of what has happened elsewhere that is no mean achievement. But it is by no means a unique achievement. The fact is that, in this entire post-war period, no nation whose people were genuinely experienced in the business of self-government has abandoned it. The traditional democracies of Europe have been under greater pressure—internal and external—than that of the United States. But, up to the present, no traditional democracy has ceased to be democratic. The

anti-democratic movement has made significant head-
way only in those states—Germany, Italy and Russia
the most notable among them—where neither the temper nor the practice of democracy was deeply ingrained.
Our democracy has come through like that of all habitually democratic nations.

Mr. Roosevelt describes the process by which he has
brought it through as "making democracy work." That,
I think, is a sales argument rather than an accurate de-
scription of what has happened.

It is a mistake to appraise the health of a democracy
entirely in terms of the democratic mechanism, or to
assume that self-government is being weakened only
when the actual instruments and institutions of self-government are under attack. Democracy, as I have pointed
out, is more than a mechanism. It is a temper, a habit,
an accumulation of inclinations, all of which have grown
out of the long-time and successful practice of self-
government. Mr. Roosevelt has been concerned for the
mechanism of democracy. He has been less concerned
for the practice of democracy. He has not greatly
changed our institutions. But I think he may change
our habits.

It is also a mistake to assume that Fascism and Communism are the only alternatives to the American type of
government. There are many alternatives. Most of
them would probably be less obnoxious than Fascism
and Communism as they are practiced in Europe, but

they would still be different from democracy as it has been practiced in the United States. Moreover, it is also true that Fascism or Communism, if we were to go in for one or the other of them, would be adapted, Americanized and made more indigenous, if not more pleasant, than the European brand. It is possible that we would call it by another name and think that we had something else altogether.

It is not my belief that Mr. Roosevelt has started us, in name or in fact, toward Fascism or Communism. So far as his conscious political objectives are concerned— I am very sure that he does not believe he has started us toward anything that differs from what we have had. His philosophy is in the American tradition and it is backed by a very considerable knowledge of American history. But because his mind works best when it has objective material to work with, his knowledge of American history is very largely a matter of facts. He has an enormous fund of interesting, historical details at his command.

As I have previously pointed out, however, Mr. Roosevelt is not—and probably lays no claim to being— a profound student of democracy. His mind is not sufficiently reflective. He knows the facts of what the democratic mood and temper have produced in the United States. I do not think he has an equal knowledge of the less tangible forces that produced the mind and temper and that condition their effectiveness. When he speaks about "making democracy work" or declares that "in the United States democracy has not had to take a holiday" he is undoubtedly thinking in terms of our definite, objective institutions. That is why he is a better defender of the machinery than of the practice of self-government. And it is the practice of self-government that is more likely to be impaired.

Traditionally, in the American system, the Congress and the Chief Executive are independent, each equally representative of the people and equally responsible for the laws which govern them. It has been our practice to rely for order and progress upon coöperation between the two rather than upon the ascendancy of one over the other. We have believed that the ascendancy of one over the other, if long continued, would inevitably threaten our political freedom. Moreover, save in emergencies, we have never had complete unanimity between the two or believed that such unanimity was desirable. Disagreement has been as important a part of our deliberative process as agreement. And however much the White House or Congress has "played politics," insisted on party regularity, and used the spoils system to enforce it, the general public, when really important issues were at stake, has looked with disfavor upon attempts, on either side, to use force on an opposition against which arguments have not prevailed.

The practice of deliberative government has been maintained by this process of give-and-take. And the practice of deliberative government, because it has involved the wholesale airing of the views of all parties to a disputed issue, has helped to lift the level of the nation's political intelligence and to make the government somewhat more representative of the considered opinions of the people. It is clear that any political development which tended frequently to short-cut this process would tend, eventually, to curtail its benefits.

On the basis of any objective appraisal both the First and the Second New Deals will be found, I believe, to constitute such a development. If the practice of deliberative government has not been impaired it is not because proposals and tactics which would have impaired it have been lacking.

Mr. Roosevelt has spoken of himself, in his relationship to the government, as a quarter back. It might be more accurate to describe him, in terms of professional baseball, as a playing manager. He is in the game with the rest of them. But he is the boss. He determines the strategy, directs the playing and proposes to fire and hire the players.

The government run that way may be representative. Mr. Roosevelt has three elections to his credit to prove that it is. But it is not deliberative. It is personal. It is leadership government of the kind familiar in Fascist states but operating—unlike Fascism—within the democratic structure. That room for the leadership principle has been found in our traditional democratic structure does not alter the fact that the principle, itself, is not a part of our traditional democracy. This may or may not be a better way for us to do business. At least it is a different way.

During the first Roosevelt administration and the First New Deal such an innovation was probably inevitable. It was made inevitable by two facts: the personality of Mr. Roosevelt, himself, and the emergency which hung over the nation when he came into office. A less aggressive and less agreeable personality than Mr. Roosevelt's could not have brought it about even in an emergency. But without the emergency even Mr. Roosevelt could probably not have managed it. In 1932, however, personality and emergency met and the combination was irresistible. Since then, in every area up to the massive doors of the Supreme Court building we have had personal government.

It was no departure from our accustomed procedure to grant great powers to the President in the crisis of 1933. It has been approved American practice, at such times, to speed up our government mechanism by suspending, to some degree, the practice of deliberation and by granting to the President powers which, in normal times, he would not be permitted to exercise. The fact that, in this crisis, more of this authority was centered in and exercised by the White House was due to Mr. Roosevelt's personality, to the unpredictable nature of the emergency, and to the immediate success which attended the President's attempts to master it.

But personal government did not pass with the crisis. The leadership principle, invoked for emergency purposes, was not surrendered. On the contrary, it was acclimated to the White House and accepted on Capitol Hill. As a result, during Mr. Roosevelt's first administration the machinery of government worked at much more than normal speed and a great many worth-while things were accomplished which deliberative government, in so short a time, could not have achieved.

If Congress had been given its head in 1933 and 1934 it would probably still be debating the measures which the President proposed in those years. But Congress was not given its head. In consequence, the 73rd Congress which met for only three months in the spring of 1933 and for only five months in the winter and spring of 1934 passed seventy measures which not only provided for the national revenue, increased the size of the navy and gave the Philippines their independence, but established the whole structure and framework of the New Deal. Only a President who was, in effect, his own legislature could have brought so much to pass so quickly.

But crisis pressure cannot explain Mr. Roosevelt's success in continuing his emergency authority beyond the emergency. His own temperament, his relish for large-scale action, his impatience, his confidence in himself indicate, of course, a mind to which personal government is peculiarly congenial. But to maintain that kind of government required more than a willing mind. Mr. Roosevelt has maintained it largely because of his own personality and by his unrivaled power with the public.

That Mr. Roosevelt's program, up to the Supreme Court issue, was put through the Congressional filter without being filtered is due, first of all, to the magic of his personality.

It is probably safe to say that during 1933, 1934 and 1935 a record-breaking number of men of some political eminence went to the President's office in a state of incipient revolt and left it to declare to the world their subscription to things that they did not subscribe to. I once met the late Senator Huey Long after such a White House love feast. The Senator said:

"I'm never going back to that place again."

I wanted to know why. He told me:

"I always feel when I leave like a man who's been sold an order of goods he hasn't any use for. I don't like the feeling and I'm not going back."

A good many people must have come away from the President and after the glow wore off have had the same sheepish feeling. The important point, however, is not the way they felt about the goods but the fact that they took the order. No salesman comparable to Mr. Roosevelt has ever sat in the President's chair and the best evidence of his salesmanship is the remarkable number of old-order conservatives who have taken on and decked themselves out in his liberalism. History will record the valiant and loyal battling for (to the conservative mind) radical measures by such men as John Garner and the late Joe Robinson and Pat Harrison, as evidence of a major selling miracle.

This procedure, made eminently successful by the melting and healing warmth of the President's personality, appeared to be in the best democratic tradition. The democratic tradition is all on the side of progress hammered out by the meeting of great minds. But, however great the minds, it would be inaccurate to say that, in these conferences, they met. It is even inaccurate to call many of their meetings conferences.

The main items in the President's program, down to the present, are not the product of consultation with those whom he expects to make them into law. His practice, rather, is to make up his own mind as to what he wants and then—if necessary—to call in his legislators, not to get their advice, but to get his orders. The success of their meeting is not that they are made to feel that they have a part in shaping what is proposed but in the fact that they are made to feel good about the acceptance of something which they have had no hand in proposing.

Most New Deal measures were drawn up without benefit of Congressional advice and counsel and, more often than not were as much of a surprise on Capitol

Hill as in the country. It happens, incidentally, that Congress has a staff of experts whose business it is to draft bills for passage. The Senator or Representative or the government agency, with a legislative idea, merely turns the idea over to the drafting department and it comes out in a bill for proper presentation to the House or Senate. Little New Deal legislation was subjected to this operation. Since the ideas, in large part, originated a long way from Capitol Hill, it was not left for Capitol Hill to prepare them for passage. In many instances, as the members of Congress will testify, the administration's advisers and aides did a very good job. In some instances they botched it badly. In either case, the job was taken over by the White House.

The ideas back of the legislation were not often Congressional and Senators and Representatives were seldom called in to aid in their development. Thus, the Triple A was chiefly a product of the minds of Henry Wallace, Rexford Guy Tugwell, and a few farm organization leaders; the National Industrial Recovery Act bore the imprint of General Hugh Johnson and his associate Alexander Sachs, a Wall street economist. The Securities Exchange Act was written, in the main, by Ben Cohen, a young lawyer in the Department of the Interior, who has since attained fame as the back-stage member of the President's highly influential team of Corcoran and Cohen. The Utilities Act was largely a Corcoran-Cohen creation. The President's now pending proposal for the reorganization of government departments was a product of the exhaustive researches of a special committee headed by Louis Brownlow of the University of Chicago. Although the Senate had its own reorganization committee under the chairmanship of Senator Byrd of Virginia, the proposals which the President finally made took no account of the likewise exhaustive investigations of that committee and came— to quote the press—"as a bomb-shell."

The measure for the reform of the judiciary and the increase in the membership of the Supreme Court was kept a deep, dark secret until the day before it was sent to the Capitol for action. On that day a number of Democratic leaders in the House and Senate were invited to attend a special meeting of the Cabinet. At that meeting Mr. Roosevelt not merely declared what he proposed to do. He read the completed bill and the finished and final draft of the message transmitting it to Congress and called on his leaders to pass it. There was nothing that the assembled leaders could do about it, at that stage, but to buckle down to the difficult business of getting it passed which, loyally as usual, they proceeded to do.

This particular bill, when it finally appeared, had no birth certificate attached. All the facts, however, seem to indicate that here, again, the brilliant young team of Corcoran and Cohen was largely responsible. One thing, however, is known certainly: the consultations out of which the measure evolved did not include the Congressional leaders upon whom, in the end, responsibility for enacting it was due to rest.

Thus Mr. Roosevelt has been and, apparently, proposes to continue to be his own legislature. There may be something to be said for this modification of our traditional practices. But there is no reason to ignore the fact that it is a modification.

But with due allowance for Mr. Roosevelt's friendliness, it is perfectly clear that this could not have come about merely as a result of the President's affability with the various members of Congress who, from time to time, lunched at his office desk. Their readiness to swallow what the President had to offer was much more than a tribute to his hospitality. It was an indication of concern for their own political hides. If what they had to swallow sometimes looked and tasted like castor oil, there was no visible Black Shirt army to force it down their throats. But they took it, none-the-less and for much the same reason. The President's thoughtfulness and charm may have made the taking easier. But a very healthy and robust fear made it inevitable. This fear, too, was partly a product of the President's personality. It was a result of a well-founded belief in the President's power with the public—a power that could be turned off or on at will to punish or to reward.

Early in March 1933, Mr. Roosevelt made the first of his historic fireside talks to "my friends," the American people. They were reassuring, explanatory, intimate. The nation was taken into the President's confidence. Doubts were dispelled, confusion routed and the public's confidence helped back toward normal. This was a significant contribution and only Mr. Roosevelt could have made it so significantly.

It does not minimize that contribution to recognize the fact that these talks soon came to serve a more directly political purpose. I am very sure that Mr. Roosevelt, at the beginning of his first administration, had no idea of his own radio powers or that he guessed the extraordinary popular reaction that they would arouse. He was not left long in doubt about it. The morning after such an address to the nation his desk would be piled with hundreds of telegrams and the White House mail room flooded.

The White House mail is sorted in the basement of the Executive offices. During previous administrations one elderly mail clerk and a couple of assistants have managed, comfortably, to handle it. With the coming of Mr. Roosevelt, however, and with his encouragement to the people of the country to write to him, the mail room suddenly came to life. New clerks were hastily added and then more new clerks. The room itself was enlarged and then enlarged again. The elderly clerk in charge finally found himself with fifteen assistants and still rushed. After a Presidential talk his staff was sometimes increased to twice that size.

The United States Changes Streams

What was happening in the White House mail room was under way, also, on Capitol Hill. I have heard it said that the day's mail of the average Senator or Representative has more than doubled during the Roosevelt administration. Evidently a good many people—having been urged by the President to write their opinions to him—decided to make a good job of it and give their Congressmen a broadside or two. At any rate, with every Presidential broadcast this flood of mail to the Capitol was increased. Senators and Representatives began to complain that—with their scant secretarial allowances—they were unable to handle this correspondence. A number of them inserted blanket apologies to their constituents in the Congressional Record and then mailed the Record out, in quantity, to their districts and states.

But no one who, during the First New Deal, watched the arrival of these letters from constituents in the office of a member of Congress can doubt that they were read and, even if they were not promptly answered, they served as amazingly effective aids to the transfer of power from Congress to the White House. Veterans in the Senate and the House, and even more the newcomers, suddenly realized that their constituents were exclusively theirs no longer; that they were more definitely the constituents of the man in the White House. They were aware, too, that the man in the White House was not going through "military channels" either in making appeals to the people or in finding out what

[87]

they were thinking. He was going over the heads of Congress. When Senators or Representatives were called to the President's office they were seldom asked—as they had been asked in previous administrations—about the state of the public mind in their particular areas. They were told what the state of the public mind in those areas was.

Word got around on Capitol Hill that "the President knows more about our constituents than we do." This was disquieting. The run-of-the-mill politician took the cue, sidetracked his own judgment and did what he was told. The politician with tendencies toward independent thinking, was forced to think twice before he indulged himself in the luxury of nonconformity.

Now, the President in his appeals to the people was not starting something new. Presidents had "gone to the country" before. The most famous instance, doubtless, was Mr. Wilson's tour in support of the League of Nations. But apart from the fact of Mr. Roosevelt's radio genius, his appeals differ from those of his predecessors in one important respect. Previous Presidents appealed on specific issues and in order to get favorable or unfavorable action on a specific measure. With some exceptions—the Supreme Court issue being the most notable of them—Mr. Roosevelt has not gone to the country primarily to stir up action, one way or the other, on a pending measure. He has gone to the country with some regularity and regardless of whether Congress was in session. The net result of his appeals has not been the passage of this particular bill or the defeat of that one. It has been, rather, to mobilize such a powerful and aggressive opinion behind himself as to insure the passage or defeat of anything that he suggested or opposed.

His talks, in other words, secure for him a blanket mandate or what, in view of his own mail and that on Capitol Hill, had all the appearances of a blanket mandate. The popular conviction came to be: "if the President is for it we are for it." It was not because of the particular issues involved that recalcitrant Senators and Representatives were condemned by their constituents, but for "opposing the President." It was not because regular Senators and Representatives had weighed the issues that they were praised but for "voting with the President."

It was almost inevitable, therefore, that Congress should not give too much thought to the surrender of its deliberative function. What the public chiefly wanted to know about a question was whether the President approved or disapproved. And politics being what it is, that was about all that Congress wanted to know. The mass mind of Congress was made up, not on Capitol Hill, but at the White House.

When Maury Maverick, one of the ablest younger Representatives in Congress, grabbed a copy of the President's Supreme Court measure from his desk, got a jump on the leaders, and introduced it as his bill he indicated how far personal government had gone. Mr. Maverick, I believe, had never read the bill or even seen it. He only recognized that it was a White House measure. That was argument enough. The fact that the path of this particular New Deal proposal was less smooth than that of any that came before it was indicative of its more drastic nature rather than of a decline in personal government.

There were, of course, occasional rumors of Congressional unrest during Mr. Roosevelt's first term. But they never materialized in anything substantial. In fact, every spring, beginning with 1934 and always coinciding with the President's fishing absences from Washington, Congress has made some show of marching its soldiers up the hill. And every spring, on the President's return, Congress had marched them down again. Mr. Roosevelt undoubtedly enjoyed these little sallies and quick retreats. And every year, up to 1937, the game ended promptly when he said: "boo."

During the fanaticism of the 1936 campaign a good many Republicans vented their hostility to Mr. Roosevelt by ridiculing his radio charm—as though his voice and personality, alone, accounted for his hold on the masses of the people. Back of their irritation at Mr. Roosevelt's speaking ability there seemed to be an ungratified yearning for a candidate with relatively equal oratorical powers. But the Republicans needed more than oratory. They needed a program. And the appeal of Mr. Roosevelt's oratory derived its greatest strength from the nature of Mr. Roosevelt's program. It is true that, from the standpoint of speaking technique, he said things the way they ought to be said. But it is also true, and more important, that what he had to say was what vast numbers of people wanted to hear. That fact, far more than his voice and manner, explains why he has been able to get blanket mandates from the people—not only at elections—but in those extra-constitutional referenda which he has conducted on the radio.

That explains, also, why a large number of people, in politics and out of it, who were accustomed to do their own thinking and vote their own convictions, found it easy to join in support of the President with those who were stampeded. The President's program, some of them argued, was the liberal program. Liberalism had had a good many lean years. The important thing—now that it appeared to be coming into its own—was to avoid quibbles and hairsplitting and go along with the President.

This was realistic liberal strategy, and liberals are not notably realistic. I believe that it was sound strategy. It seems to me that most of the liberal eggs, in 1936, were in the Roosevelt basket. A government based on the leadership principle may or may not be an accepted liberal doctrine. But—in 1936—the Second New Deal was not on the horizon and personal government had not been offered as an administration program.

It was not yet apparent that the Roosevelt plan to hatch the liberals' eggs was to be advocated as a permanent modification of our incubation procedure. That fact did not become apparent until, in the spring of 1937, the President launched the Second New Deal. The measures of the Second New Deal, unlike those of the First, were not the products of an emergency and they were not suggested as temporary expedients. It is true that the President, in one of his radio speeches in support of the Court plan, rang the familiar changes on the necessity for action "now" and offered a dire picture of what, action failing, was about to happen. But that appeal was intended to stir up the animals and not to give the idea that what the President was asking for—on the Court or anything else—was merely for the duration of "the crisis." The President, at the 1937 session of Congress, did not present crisis legislation, however much a crisis psychology was invoked to get it passed. What he offered was a long-time program for the nation.

That fact is a partial explanation for the opposition that has arisen on Capitol Hill. In the spring of 1933, a good many men voted for a good many things that they did not particularly believe in simply because of what appeared to be the prevailing darkness. This number not only included many Republicans, but doubting Democrats like Senators Glass and Byrd of Virginia, Walsh of Massachusetts, Bailey of North Carolina, Tydings of Maryland, and Clark of Missouri. The spring of 1937, however, had a very different look. The President undoubtedly expected and was not particularly troubled by the prospect of opposition from those whose previous support had been because of the emergency rather than by conviction.

But the Second New Deal differs from the First, not only because it has no emergency excuse, but because it has a different purpose. The measures of 1933 and thereafter had to do, chiefly, with the nation's economic structure. The measures of 1937, however much they may be appealed for on economic grounds, have also to do with the nation's political practices. Their chief significance does not lie in the fact that they involve the repair of economic damage or the remedy of economic abuses, but in the fact that they serve to put executive government on a permanent basis. For some time the tendency has been to center more and more authority in Washington. The Second New Deal goes much further than that and centers authority in the White House.

It is not, therefore, opposition to any specific proposal but a growing realization that this is the objective of all of these measures that accounts for the insurgency of many heretofore administration regulars and the undercover uneasiness of a much larger number who have not yet spoken up. A good many members of Congress who were convinced that the nation's economic system needed overhauling will not concede that its political practices need to be changed. All of the President's

recently introduced and so-called "key proposals"
plainly involve such a change.

The Supreme Court measure is the most familiar type
of this kind of legislation. It was offered as a measure
to make the Court more sensitive to the need for economic readjustment. If that had been the whole story
the plan would probably have gone through with few
hitches. But it was more than that. Senatorial liberals
like Wheeler and O'Mahoney and Van Nuys opposed
the plan, not because they were against any plan to
"reform" the Court, but because this measure made the
Court subject to the will and pleasure of the White
House.

Moreover, the method which the proposal presented
was even more ominously suggestive of the President's
purposes than the contents of the bill, itself. Here, as I
indicated in the previous chapter, was a measure which,
on the face of it, involved a fundamental revision in the
set-up of the American government. But the people
were not asked to pass on it. The only will that was consulted was the will of the President.

I happen to know that at least one of Mr. Roosevelt's
most devoted friends in Congress pled long with him,
and unavailingly, to submit the question, through an
amendment, to the nation and promised his aggressive
support to get such an amendment ratified. But the
President, who relied on his blanket mandate as authori-
zation for such a plan, apparently did not have confi-

dence enough in either the plan or the mandate to submit it to any such test.

The President's other Second New Deal measures were equally revealing. Almost every one in Congress believes, for example, that some sort of Federal reorganization is desirable and necessary. But the President's plan for reorganization is much more than that. It involves the surrender to the White House of the independence of such boards and commissions as the Interstate Commerce Commission and the Federal Trade Commission, gives the President new power to control the Civil Service, vests in him, instead of in Congress, authority over most of the Federal budget, gives him power to abolish governmental agencies and create new ones and makes it impossible for the House and Senate to override him in these matters with anything less than a two-thirds vote. When, therefore, Senator Byrd of Virginia leads what is likely to be at least a partially successful fight against this plan—it will not be because he is against reorganization, but because this plan of reorganization involved an unparalleled extension of White House government.

Similarly, the President's first draft of a wages and hours bill was not looked upon with such wide disfavor in Congress because Congress is opposed to legislation on wages and hours. A substantial Congressional majority is not opposed to such legislation. But the President's measure as it first appeared was much more than that.

[95]

His bill would have centered authority over wages, hours, and production, that is, over the nation's economic life, in the hands of a five man board which means, in effect, that it would have been centered in the President, since the board is appointed by and answerable to him.

The White House policy on relief fits nicely into the same picture. Most of the members of Congress believe in economy, but very few of them believe that the time has arrived for the government to get entirely out of the relief business. A proposal was recently presented in the Senate to make the localities share, in so far as they are able, from 25 to 40 per cent of the Federal government's relief bill.

Senators Byrnes and Robinson and the Democrats who voted with them and against the administration on this proposal did not offer their plan as a way whereby the government could get out from under. They proposed it as a step toward the more equitable distribution of the relief burden. But back of that was a desire, in line with their states rights convictions, to begin to get relief out of Washington and back to the localities. And back of the administration's opposition was its determination to continue the centralized, White House control over both the funds and the manner of their expenditure.

It is not only the specific measures of the Second New Deal that indicates the tendency toward personal, White House government. That tendency is even more definitely indicated by the tactics which have been employed to secure the enactments of those measures. On the Supreme Court issue Mr. Roosevelt ran into his first serious legislative snag. He was, in fact, confronted with a situation where personal government required more than the persuasive powers and previously appealing policies of the President. Even the threat of radio speeches and the actual speeches themselves appeared, on this issue at least, to work less magic. Personal government needed as—sooner or later—it always needs an enforcement mechanism. Such a mechanism was found in the national Democratic organization.

Party organizations in the past have existed to put men in office and to keep them there. They have not, heretofore, assumed legislative responsibility. The President is the head of the national organization of his party. But it has not been the custom in the past for Presidents to make personal use of the party machinery as a propagandist agency with the people and a punitive instrument against the people's elected representatives.

But in this situation the Democratic national organization took over this additional function. With the apparent approval of Mr. Roosevelt and under the direct leadership of Mr. Farley the Democratic National Committee was used to make a weapon, offensive and defensive, for short-cutting our traditional deliberative practice. It became the Black Shirt army for the administration's castor oil.

Charlie Michelson, old, dour, and mysterious, who probably returned from his post-election vacation looking forward to a long breathing spell was obliged, overnight, to jump back into the campaign again. He had the publicity organization. All he had to do was to start it going. He did. The radio division was manned by the same person who manned it during the campaign. Michelson's desk was loaded—as it had been in the campaign—with literature, in manuscript and in proof. The committee's storeroom was stacked with Supreme Court pamphlets and folders. Charlie, himself, had to return to long hours at the typewriter producing material for publication and writing speeches for the various administration orators. And an alert observer, posted outside the National Press Building, could have seen Tom Corcoran on almost any day during the height of the Court fight, making a beaten path between the White House and the offices of the National Committee.

The brunt of the out-in-front work, of course, was borne by Mr. Farley. "Jim," had planned to retire from the Cabinet shortly after the 4th of March and take a remunerative job in private business. But he postponed his retirement until the end of the new campaign. A crop of new post offices in strategically important states suddenly were found in need of dedication and Mr. Farley assumed the onerous task of chief dedicator, with the Supreme Court issue as the burden of his dedicatory remarks.

He traveled widely, north, south, east, and west. Wherever he went he met the party's state and local leaders. It can be assumed that his consultations with them were not merely reminiscences of the 1936 campaign. And it goes without saying that many a Capitol Hill dignitary, aware that the Chairman had arrived in his bailiwick, trembled in his boots and began to wonder whether, after all, it would not be the wisest course to support the President's policy.

It was in the midst of such salutary campaigning that Mr. Farley, who although an able public servant is not a legislator, publicly declared "we have the votes." The importance of that declaration is not in the degree of its accuracy, but in the fact that it indicates the establishment, in Washington, of a new type of legislative lobby—a Presidential lobby, working through the party organization to bring pressure to bear on legislators, and, pressure failing, to take steps in the legislators' districts to mete out punishment.

Just how clearly this is understood in those districts is indicated by an incident that followed the 1937 meeting in Oklahoma City of the General Federation of Women's Clubs. The assembled women voted their disapproval of the President's Supreme Court plan. The move to take such action was fought, hard and long, by Oklahoma's Democratic National Committeewoman. After her efforts to stop the vote were defeated she declared to the newspapermen, with obvious foreboding:

"When I go to Washington to try to get projects for Oklahoma, they'll say 'you let the President get slapped in the face down there in Oklahoma.' "

This fear of the punitive operations of the party's political machine was not notably successful in the Supreme Court fight. The Senate, on that issue and despite the danger involved, dared to resume its deliberative function. But the fact that the party machine was thrown into action to frighten an opposition that could not be persuaded indicates a considerable departure from our accustomed regard for deliberative practices.

Perhaps, for an impatient people, pressed by a large number of unsolved problems and unremedied iniquities, this current tendency to short-cut democracy is desirable. On the other hand, the practice of short-cuts may become habitual and the establishment of personal government within the structure of representative government may lead to its acceptance in the place of representative government.

Meanwhile, it is likely that Mr. Roosevelt, whether he is President for only two terms or for three, will continue to insist upon this modification of our system. He is too deeply committed to it; by nature, he finds it too much to his liking and, from the practical point of view of what he still desires to accomplish, he is too certain that there is no expeditious alternative. But personal government is due to meet increasing opposition, not only outside, but within, the President's own party.

If the President overcomes that opposition it will be because he has maintained his leadership of those non-party forces which the First New Deal mobilized, upon which the Second New Deal clearly depends and whose mounting power bids fair to change, entirely, the political map of the nation.

CHAPTER V

THE SELF-PERPETUATING NEW DEAL

THERE is probably only one thing that could defeat Mr. Roosevelt if he should choose to run for President in 1940. That one thing is a third party with its own Presidential ticket and enough support to divide the New Deal vote. But a third party could never get that much support unless, far from opposing the New Deal, it promised to outdeal it. The New Deal, as against any lesser program, is unbeatable. It is the nearest thing to a self-perpetuating government that the United States has ever seen.

This is true for two reasons. First, because of what Mr. Roosevelt has done, is doing and proposes to continue to do for those millions of Americans whose average annual incomes are less than $2000. Second, because of its program of education, propaganda, and organization by which the millions benefited are made aware of the benefits and of the ways and means by which they can be guarded and increased. These two facts, and the political forces they released, elected Mr. Roosevelt in 1936. Unless he should weary of reform, curtail his program and open the way for a third party to outbid the New Deal, they would elect him again in 1940. Self-interest is more potent at the polls than precedent.

Mr. Roosevelt, during his first term of office, helped a great many people. He whetted a great many appetites. Most important of all, he has helped the appetites to organize.

It is a mistake to say that the President, on the morning after the 1936 election, was a free man with debts to no one. He was loaded down with debts. For election purposes, what he had accomplished in four years for labor, for agriculture, for the unemployed, and the under-privileged was no less significant than what he repeatedly declared ought to be accomplished. His fighting speech at Madison Square Guarden—which I believe he regarded as the most effective speech of his campaign—was not an invitation to these special groups to vote for him because of what he had done, but because of what he promised to do. They took him at his word and voted for him. The historic fact about the 1936 election was not that the President carried so many states, but that he carried so many classes.

Thus, when John L. Lewis, in the spring of 1937, publicly presented the bill for the class he represents, the President had no alternative but to honor it. The

Era of Good Feeling was not deliberately abandoned. It simply disappeared under a flood of such bills.

The special interests which were most influential in Washington in the palmy days of Wall Street Republicanism did most of their wirepulling behind the scenes and most of their gumshoeing after nightfall in the dim, upholstered reaches of the Willard, the Mayflower and the Shoreham. There is nothing clandestine about the special interests which have more recently taken over. They could not afford the luxury even if it were required. But it is not required. What they are out to get the President has encouraged them to seek. They, therefore, can seek it openly.

That is all to the good. It seems to me for example that the open and aboveboard and very much stormed against marches of the WPA to the Capitol are far less dangerous than the undercover finaglings of those who use luxurious hotel suites as their base and lavish parties as their bait. Moreover, the right of these political newcomers to a larger place in the economic sun is undoubtedly more valid than that of the veteran fixers who thrived in the Republican era. The mass lobbyists of the Roosevelt administration may be unwise in some of the things they ask for, uncouth in the way they ask for them, and cocky about the consequences. But there is more basic justice in their demands. They are out to get what they have had too little of. The Harding-Coolidge-Hoover fixers were out to guard and to increase what they already had too much of. So far as the legitimate needs of those for whom he speaks are concerned, John L. Lewis has a better claim to consideration at the White House than Thomas Lamont.

But there is more involved here than the rights of those who have been presenting their requisitions. Up to the present, the debate with Mr. Roosevelt has been largely on economic grounds. But politics is involved. And in the long run the political issue is likely to over shadow the economic issue and to determine it. For the President, through his economic reforms, has prepared the way for a political revolution which will be no less drastic because it probably will be peaceful.

Mr. Roosevelt has served the special interests of certain classes of our citizens. It was undoubtedly high time that somebody served them. But he has done more than that. He has used the machinery of the government of the United States to organize those classes on behalf of their special interests. There is no mystery as to why he did this. His economic reform, like democratic undertakings of any sort, had to have political support. It is altogether possible that in the long run the particular kind of support which he has encouraged may be more of a threat to the reforms than a safeguard. But the extent to which the government machinery has been used to drum it up and to organize it is something new under our political sun. It is that which makes the New Deal, at least for the immediate future, virtually self-perpetuating. Political parties are at as much of a disadvantage in competition with the government as private business enterprise.

It is one of those fortuitous circumstances which turn up, now and then, that there has been no conflict among the New Dealers between social vision and political necessity. The politics of the New Deal is no less congenial than its humanitarianism. The things which, for expediency's sake, they have had to do were the very things which they would have chosen to do.

After the first emergency period passed, it was clear that the New Deal could continue and expand only if pressure for its continuance and expansion was organized by insiders and on the inside. The Democratic Party was not an acceptable vehicle for such an organization. The Party machinery was not New Deal machinery. A good many of the most potent figures in it had very little idea what all the New Deal fuss and fury was about and a good many others, who did know, definitely disapproved.

Moreover, neither the spirit nor the personnel of the First New Deal was particularly Democratic. Most of the young men and women who swarmed into Washington and made the fine frenzy of 1933 and 1934 were attached to many things. But the Democratic Party was not one of them. To them it was as moribund as capitalism, and for the same reasons. The political orthodoxy of their superiors was just as dubious. Much of the shining armor of those days would have gone dull if the idea had ever got around that this crusade had to be kept inside the party's fences. But that idea never went around and the fences were ignored.

Unlike previous political movements in the United States, therefore, the New Deal was neither Democratic nor Republican. It did not need to be. The economic policies of the New Deal were better stuff out of which to build a political defense than any political party could provide.

From the fourth of March 1933, to the first of July 1937, Mr. Roosevelt has spent eight to ten billion dollars over and above what can be reckoned as the normal cost of running the national government in addition to the bonus payment and allowing for recoverable assets. In other words, this is the non-collectible emergency total. Most of these billions were disbursed, directly or indirectly, as benefit payments to individual American citizens.

There is no way of knowing exactly how many people were on the receiving end. Leaving out of account the millions who have been and are on Federal relief, the direct and indirect beneficiaries probably numbered not less than 50,000,000 people. Including the relief totals the number would undoubtedly exceed 60,000,000. That is, Mr. Roosevelt, during his first four and a half years, put half the population of the United States under material obligation to the New Deal. In half the families of

America it was possible to point to some definite benefit and say: "Mr. Roosevelt gave us that."

Then from the political point of view, the nature of the benefits was just as significant as the vast number of them. The New Deal spent a comparatively small part of its total expenditures as direct cash payments. The United States did not generally resort to the dole. I think that the reasons for the administration's refusal to resort to the dole were sound reasons. A dole policy would have cost much less in immediate financial outlay. But the long-run cost, in terms of the deterioration of morale, would probably have been considerably more.

But on the political side, if we had had the dole we could not have had the New Deal. The money which we have spent not only financed us through and out of the depression. It financed us into the New Deal. Our determination to make our expenditures productive has produced human and material benefits which seem to me to justify the policy. But it also produced political results which—however desirable—are likely to be of greater long-time significance. Socially, we have produced morale and bridges and educations and higher farm prices and cheaper electric rates and a whole multitude of good things. Politically, we have produced a new attitude toward the government and a new movement—entirely outside the existing parties—through which to make that attitude effective.

The attitude is a direct result of the fact that the administration's spending was not merely to keep our hard-hit citizens from starvation. The administration went much beyond that. It has undertaken to finance their ambitions and to pay for their hopes. This may be desirable. It may be the inevitable result of a hastily built economic order, too many of whose builders delayed too long to do, voluntarily, the things which Washington is now attempting. But however desirable and inevitable, the fact remains that it is altering what has been the traditional American attitude toward our government. We have looked to the government in the United States to guard the individual's freedom of opportunity. We have more recently begun to look to it to protect the individual from the worst consequences of his lack of opportunity. During the last four and a half years, however, we have gone much farther. We have now begun to expect that the government should create our opportunities.

This is being written just after the Commencement season. During the past few week a good many thousands of young people have graduated from our high schools and colleges. Approximately one in every five of the members of the Class of 1937 will have been helped diploma-ward by Washington. In 1936, 280,000 high school boys and girls received pocket money from the National Youth Administration for car-fare, lunches, textbooks. In that year the N.Y.A. aided nearly 400,000 high school and college students. That fact undoubtedly makes Aubrey Williams, the director of the N.Y.A., the most influential schoolman in history. But it also indicates how times have changed. Aubrey Williams finished his education with a doctorate at the University of Bordeaux. But he started it in a Y.M.C.A. night school.

Between the first of October 1935, and the first of May 1937, more than 57,000,000 people attended the 80,000 concerts given by WPA musicians under the Federal Music Project. On the first of May 1937, more than half a million persons were receiving free music lessons from WPA music teachers. More than 7 million free lessons had been given in New York City alone. The same project has financed composers who, in that time, have produced 4915 original compositions. Forty-five cities have WPA symphony orchestras and 110 cities orchestras of more than 35 players.

The cultural benefits of this undertaking are of incalculable value. There is no evidence whatsoever that music financed by the government is in any degree inferior in quality or less salutary in effect than music provided in any other way. Moreover, with the government financing our musical life a far greater number of people than ever before are able to enjoy or have an active part in it. Perhaps these cultural advantages entirely outweigh any political consequences. But the fact still remains that a governmentally financed culture—however good the culture—is something new in the way of government. And the political attitude of a people who get their culture that way—however successfully they get it—is certain to be a different attitude from that which has prevailed in the past.

Probably the most dramatic and certainly the most intensive of the New Deal's undertakings in the field of social pioneering has been under the Tennessee Valley Authority. The main task of the TVA, of course, was the lowering of electrical rates. It has done that and in the wake of low-cost electrical power its engineers have turned out a whole factory-full of new gadgets for the use and comfort of the residents of the Valley. They have developed an electric hotbed for flowers and vegetables; an electric hay drier; an electric hay hoist; an electric brooder for the poultry plant; a plant for the "quick-freezing" of fruit; a plant for dehydrating fruit. Dr. Arthur E. Morgan of the TVA, has established "refrigerator coöperatives," in which the farmers of the region deposit a part of their various food crops and meats against the season when fresh foods, in the past, have not been available.

No one who has had any recent first-hand contact with the Tennessee Valley will deny that these vast and varied activities are actually bringing about the rehabilitation of what has been a decidedly run-down civilization. If, as the Second New Deal now proposes, there is to be a series of little TVA's across the country and if these off-spring do half the job that the parent project has accomplished, the whole nation will benefit immeasurably. Whether it will benefit politically is doubtful.

Since 1935, the Rural Electrification Administration has brought electricity to 100,000 farm homes and has a ten year program which will electrify 1,000,000 farm homes. The Resettlement Administration has helped more than 700,000 families to reëstablish themselves on a self-supporting basis. The Home Owners' Loan Corporation has negotiated loans for more than 1,000,-000 home owners. The Federal Housing Administration has aided an undetermined number of families to build new homes or repair and improve old ones. In the last four and a half years, Federally financed activities have taught 700,000 persons to read and write.

This catalogue of significant New Deal activities might be indefinitely extended. I doubt if any government ever before in so short a time undertook to do so many new things or did them so well or had so few with which a right-minded citizen could find fault. Some of them undoubtedly will be paying significant social dividends long after the debts incurred to finance them have been liquidated.

But future historians will have more than these social data to consider in their appraisal of what has been happening in this extraordinary period. They will have to consider political consequences—the effect of all that has been done upon the operation of our government.

And the first of those consequences probably will be found in the development of a new attitude toward the government.

Mr. Roosevelt's program being what it is and human nature being what it is assumed to be, such a development was, of course, inevitable. A government can hardly undertake to do the things which this government has undertaken without a consequent increase in what the people for whom the things are done expect. And, the more that is done the more is expected. This, by the way, is not a peculiarity of the under-privileged—of whom it is the customary reactionary opinion that "if you give them an inch they'll take a mile." The reactionaries ought to know. They developed that technique. I should say that the chief difference between the reactionaries and the under-privileged, at this point, is that the reactionaries got their mile.

But the present administration has not left the development of a beneficiary attitude toward the government to chance or to the normal working of human nature. It has deliberately stimulated it and helped to make it into an effective political organization—defensive and offensive. The appetites which the New Deal whetted were bound to be politically significant. But the New Deal's mobilization of those appetites is the most important political and economic development in the last seventy-five years of American history.

This new political force is independent of any party—

just as independent as the second- and third-string New Deal administrators who are chiefly responsible for having created it. For the time being its chief political attachment is to Mr. Roosevelt, personally. He has been and is the source of the benefits. But its only long-run attachment is to the benefits. If and when Mr. Roosevelt puts on the brakes these supporters are sure to cut off the gas. They are for the New Deal and will be until it begins to deal less or until some other movement appears that promises to deal more.

The process by which this mobilization has been brought about constitutes a considerable departure from what has been the customary procedure of the government of the United States. It has not been the practice, in the past, to use the government machinery to enlist support for the administration that happens to be in power. That has always been held to be the function of the party machinery. Naturally, the party in power has easier access to the facts since it had a more direct relationship with the various government departments than the opposition party. But the business of turning the facts into political propaganda and the dissemination of the propaganda have been party, not government, jobs.

It is interesting to note that, in 1913, shortly after Mr. Wilson came into office, there was a considerable discussion in the House of Representatives of the following amendment which was offered to the deficiency appropriation bill: "no money appropriated by this or any other act shall be used for the compensation of any publicity expert unless specifically appropriated for that purpose." The amendment was introduced by a Republican. But it received hearty endorsement on the Democratic side of the aisle. The debate was revealing. Representative Fitzgerald, one of the leaders of the House Democrats, declared:

"I should be very much surprised at any attempt to employ what is known as a publicity agent in any department of the government. I recollect that some years ago I was somewhat instrumental in calling the attention of the House to the fact that a publicity agent had been employed in connection with one service of the government at a compensation of $10,000 a year, which resulted in very emphatic action by Congress to prevent such employment. . . . I do not believe that any department or bureau or service should employ men to extol its virtues or its activities."

Mr. Campbell. "Mr. Chairman, I simply desire to call the attention of the gentleman from New York to the further fact, to which he has not alluded, that there have been in the departments of this government within recent months—I cannot say just when—employees paid by the government for making newspaper clippings and giving out interviews and gathering up things for the purpose of advertising the chiefs of bureaus and heads of departments."

Mr. Fitzgerald. ". . . we hope to eliminate all of

those evil practices. This provision I am convinced will prevent the possibility of the development of what I would conceive to be a very unfortunate situation in the government service."

The amendment—supported by both parties—was passed.

The letter of this law has probably been observed. At least, publicity experts have not been and are not being employed by that name. But no one questions that they are being employed—as statisticians, editors, directors of information, executive assistants, special assistants and in a variety of other more or less obvious capacities.

On December 21, 1936 the Civil Service Commission announced an examination for informational service representatives with duties as follows:

"In one of the larger regional offices of the Social Security Board to act as representative of the Informational Service; to plan and direct a program for bringing about on the part of the greatest possible number of persons in the region a thorough understanding of the provisions of the Social Security Act and of its administration, through the answering of inquiries and through informational material distributed through the press, radio, trade and professional groups and other media of public information and education; to advise the regional director and his staff on all matters of public relations."

No one will question the need of the Social Security Board for a service which will help to clarify the pro-

visions of the Social Security Act and no one will maintain that the information service of this particular government agency is in any way a unique phenomenon. In
fact, it is no phenomenon at all. A government agency
without an information service would be a phenomenon.

During the fiscal year, 1936, the various executive
agencies of the government—and not including the
WPA, paid out $521,000 in salaries for persons solely
in publicity work or a part of whose time was allocated
for that kind of work. An additional $81,000 was paid
out in salaries for publicity workers whose time was not
definitely allocated. During the three campaign months
of July, August, and September 1936, the information
services of these government agencies—still leaving out
the WPA—produced and sent out more than 7,000,000
copies of 4700 different releases.

The WPA, which probably has the largest and the
most effective information service of any government
agency, is not included in these totals because neither
for the report of the Brookings Institution nor in Harry
Hopkins' testimony before the House Committee on
Appropriations were any exact figures given.

A publicity mechanism of such size is, as I have said,
something new in our government. But it has more dis-
tinction than its size. No one, I think, will question the
desirability—as in the case of the Social Security
Board—for some effort to clarify the intricate operations of a government with which the average citizen is

required, increasingly, to do business. Neither will any-one question the work of the information service of such agencies as the National Park Service and the National Forestry Service which aim to bring the recreational advantages of our parks and forests to the attention of the people. The effect of the propaganda for those services is not political. The average visitor in a national park is almost sure to enjoy himself. But he is not likely to credit this or any particular administration for his pleasure. Our parks are a credit to the government of the United States—like the Navy or the Lighthouse Service. And that is the way they have been sold to the nation.

That, however, is not the way in which the benefits which have been inaugurated under the New Deal have been and are being sold. The information service of its agencies serve as New Deal agencies. Some of them have served a useful explanatory purpose. But almost all of them have gone in heavily for the business of selling the administration by propaganda for the particular agencies represented. In the last campaign the Democratic National Committee—as is customary—put out an ambitious series of pamphlets and folders extolling the administration in terms of the specific things it had accomplished. But those pamphlets and folders were a work of supererogation. The most helpful extolling work was being done by the propaganda of the government, itself.

The Self-perpetuating New Deal

The precedent and, to some degree, the pace for this kind of activity were set by the National Recovery Administration. Undoubtedly, the complex procedures involved in compliance with the National Industrial Recovery Act required a large-scale explanatory service of some sort. But the press section of the N.R.A. in the Department of Commerce Building was much more than an explanatory service. It was a selling service, manned by newspaper people. It was hectic, high-pressure, but exceedingly effective. Washington's working newspaper men and women flocked to it. Nobody had any doubt as to its purpose. It was out to sell the country on the N.R.A.

To supplement its work with the press, Charles F. Horner, one-time head of the Horner-Redpath Chautauquas, was called in to set up a speakers bureau. The result was a vocal blanketing of the country which was probably never before equaled in our history except in a war or a political campaign. When things got into something of a tangle and the political fruit of the N.R.A. did not appear to be properly ripening, the authorities went to the Democratic National Committee for help. The Democratic Committee "lent" the services of Charley Michelson—one of the best political ripeners in the country. If, by the 1936 election, the N.R.A. had ceased to be an issue or had become a political liability, the fault cannot be charged against its Information Service. Government money was never more generously or, in general, more effectively spent for turning a government activity to political account. The N.R.A. is dead. But so far as the mobilization of New Deal beneficiaries is concerned, the results of the N.R.A. propaganda go marching on.

But this mobilization has been helped along by more than these formal press services. The government has gone extensively into the moving picture business. The actual figures are hard to get at. It has been estimated, however, that between 1933 and 1937 between five and ten million dollars have been spent by the government in the production of motion pictures. More than forty separate Federal agencies are engaged in motion picture operations. Probably not less than 14,000,000 feet of government films are now available in Washington.

Some of these films are technical and educational and have no political significance whatsoever. But the political arguments in a good many of the others are all the more effective because they are indirect. I do not doubt the educational value of such listed films as: "Boulder Dam," "Grand Coulee Dam," "Boise Idaho Project," "Civilian Conservation Corps at Work," "Making a Better Indiana." But it is equally impossible to question their political significance. They are not only produced to show pictures. They are produced to answer questions. And since every one of these particular subjects is, to some degree, a political issue the process of answering the questions constitutes, inevitably, a political argument.

Probably the most ambitious single government film is "The Plow that Broke the Plains"—a three reel film produced by the Resettlement Administration at a cost of $40,000. Prints of this film were distributed, free of charge, to commercial motion picture theaters through the regional offices of the Resettlement Administration. Technically, "The Plow that Broke the Plains" was a well-done job. Politically, it was also significant. It was not a coincidence that the film was released in May 1936—with the Presidential campaign just about to get under way. It was perfectly natural that the authorities at Resettlement should desire to dramatize their achievements for the benefit of an administration that had made their achievements possible. The point is that, until recently, that was a new kind of an undertaking for the government.

So far as distribution is concerned, "The Plow that Broke the Plains" will probably rank lower in the scale than "We, the People, and Social Security," produced by the Social Security Board. This film had a length of only 363 feet. But 2001 prints were made of it. A notice was sent, by free post, to every motion picture theater in the United States stating that the film was available without charge. It was sent to the theaters requesting it—also without postage charges. It was returned postage collect, the amount being paid by the

Board. That this film was believed to be of political value is best indicated by the fact that it was released to the theaters on October 15th—three weeks before the election. No one, I think will decry the enthusiasm of the authorities at the Social Security Board to lend a hand to the administration that brought their important activity into being. But the fact remains that, heretofore, such activities have been held to be somewhat outside the scope of official governmental business.

The government has gone in for radio on an even more extensive scale—although the outlay has been considerably less. In fact, so far as the records show, the government has not had to purchase any radio time. Radio companies, both the chains and the local stations, are obliged to secure a renewal of their broadcasting licenses every three months. In addition to that there is a constant incipient threat that the government may take over the entire radio business. As a matter of radio policy, therefore, government requests for time on the air are seldom, if ever, refused.

In regard to networks the Office of Education in the Department of the Interior has had the greatest number of regular programs. Its dramatizations have appeared approximately five times a week on both the National and Columbia systems. These programs have not been, in any sense, political.

More important than network programs, however, has been the use of electrical transcriptions. By this method programs are put on in a studio where they are transcribed on records from which any number of recordings can then be made—very much as any number of prints can be made from a single photographic negative. The recordings are sent to local radio stations where they are put on as regular fifteen minute programs. During the last six months of 1936, some 500 stations used WPA recorded programs three times a week. This year some 570 stations are taking them once a week. These programs are largely musical. But there is always a one-minute WPA talk included in them. It is generally conceded at WPA, I believe, that it is the one minute talk that gives the recorded programs their significance.

"The objective here, as with our movies," one WPA executive told me, "is to sell the WPA spending program as a sound economic investment."

The Federal Housing Administration and the Resettlement Administration have likewise gone in heavily for recorded radio programs.

A number of the government's activities in this general field do not come under the head of the press, the movies, or the radio. Some of these will be considered in later chapters. One of the most interesting of them, however, is a project of the Office of Education for the establishment of Community Forums throughout the nation. Dr. John W. Studebaker, United States Commissioner of Education, was formerly Superintendent of Schools at Des Moines, Iowa, where he organized a very successful community forum. In Washington, in 1935, he secured an appropriation of $660,000 for the establishment of such forums on a national scale. Nineteen localities, in nineteen different states, were selected for what Dr. Studebaker calls his "laboratory forums."

Local management is in the hands of local committees, always in coöperation with the city or county board of education. The subjects to be discussed are determined locally. They almost always relate to current events: politics, economics, or foreign affairs. The formal speaking is always followed by open discussion. The speakers are chosen from a panel of speakers provided by Washington. The local director is also selected from nominations furnished by Washington. The speakers are paid, out of Dr. Studebaker's fund, from $300 to $500 a month and can count on steady employment— that is, six meetings a week—for five or six weeks. In the experimental areas, such as the county with which I am most familiar, a number of communities are included in the project with regular weekly meetings, discussion and luncheon groups running through a considerable part of the winter. It is Dr. Studebaker's plan— pending Congressional approval—to secure an appropriation for this work of $2,000,000 a year for three years. That would make possible from one to three forums areas in every state in the union.

I think it is undeniably true that Dr. Studebaker's

office uses a great deal of care in keeping this project
clear of what might be called "political implications."
A painstaking effort is made to see to it that the speakers included in the panels are chosen because of their
fitness to discuss certain topics without regard for political affiliations or leanings. Nevertheless, it is equally
true that the whole atmosphere of the project—as it
gets down to the individual locality—is one of somewhat more than half-way friendliness to the administration and the New Deal. After all, the administration
provides the funds. Furthermore, it is not likely that
many hostile anti-administration speakers would apply
for inclusion in the panels. At the actual meetings, there
is full freedom of discussion. But the leadership, the
actual speakers and, usually, the individuals who are
most active, locally, in promoting the work come from
among the friends of the New Deal. The net educational result is undoubtedly considerable. But there is
also a considerable political result.

Now, these vast governmental operations in the field
of what, in general, we can call propaganda have accomplished a number of things. For one thing, they have
made the general American public more familiar than
it has ever been before with the detailed working of its
Federal government. For another thing, they have
made it easier for that considerable number of Americans who are obliged to have dealings with the government to know what it is all about and, therefore, to deal

more intelligently. Again, these activities have probably stimulated a vast amount of political discussion, pro and con, throughout the nation and, in consequence, have helped to increase the political literacy of the people. These developments are all desirable.

There are certain other results which seem to me to be open to considerable debate. The most important of these propaganda operations have been carried on by the New Deal, as distinguished from the long-established and regular government agencies. One of their obvious aims is to "sell" the agency—to set forth with as much drama as can be mustered the need for the job that the agency is doing and the human happiness and well-being that are flowing from it. That kind of propaganda—as I have already indicated—is something new for our government. And the effect of it is, not only to sell the administration agency but to sell the administration.

Again, most of these agencies represent benefits of one kind or another. In most instances the benefits are highly desirable. Until the advent of the present administration it probably never occurred to any considerable number of the American people that the Federal government could or ever would undertake to provide all of these highly desirable things. It is true that our government has lagged behind that of other civilized governments in some of these matters. But it is also true that—now that it is in the business—the present government is educating its beneficiaries, not only in the righteousness of what they are getting but, as an inevitable corollary, in the justice of almost any claim they may put in for more.

This, I think, is unfortunate at least for two reasons. First, a government which convinces a considerable number of its citizens as to the availability of blank checks is likely to find itself without funds or, if it should attempt to stop payment, with a political upheaval on its hands. On the economic side, it does not follow that the under-privileged, because their needs are bona fide, are best qualified to determine how far and fast the government can go to meet them. On the political side, it certainly follows that after the beneficiaries have been encouraged to write their own ticket there will be more than a little trouble in store for any administration which seeks to take away the privilege.

But this mobilization of beneficiaries is unfortunate for another reason. The future of a great many desirable reforms has been entrusted, almost entirely, to those who benefit by the reforms. That, I think, puts the reforms, themselves, in peril. It puts them in peril because those who stand to gain are likely to fall into a "get while the getting is good" attitude—as the reactionaries so often did before them. In the long run extremists in the United States almost always pay with their own hides. A vast number of people, a far greater number than directly benefit by them, believe in the reforms of the Roosevelt administration. It is a misjudgment of the temper of our democracy to believe that these reforms can be permanently effective unless the support for them includes that group of unbenefited and largely middle-class citizens.

To win that support may require some not altogether satisfactory compromises. It may require some restraint. Restraint and compromise are not fighting words. But they express the democratic temper and they are the stuff out of which democratic progress has been maintained. The New Deal—as it is now organized—is bigger and more potent than any political party. With the funds and the machinery at its disposal it is—for the immediate future—virtually self-perpetuating. But it is altogether possible that the forces that insure its power, at the present, may eventually, for lack of the democratic temper, bring about its collapse.

CHAPTER VI

RELIEF ARMY WITH BANNERS

THERE is probably no machinery for the self-perpetuation of the New Deal that is comparable to that which has been set up under the Works Progress Administration. No other New Deal agency equals the WPA in the scope of its activities, the number of its contacts, and the compactness of its organization. No blame can possibly attach to those facts. The organization which Harry Hopkins and his corps of eager, forward-looking assistants have put together is the only kind of an organization for the job they have to do. It is doing that job exceedingly well. It does not detract from it to point out that some of the fruit of its work is political.

As head of the WPA, Harry Hopkins presides over the biggest administrative undertaking in the peace-time history of the American government. Barring unforeseen and unlikely scandals, he is due to leave it— when he finally takes his wife's advice—with a record that will match the size of the undertaking. The WPA has been widely hated and condemned. But the hatred and condemnation have seldom been supported by anything more than hearsay: "A friend of mine knows the person who saw this happen." The fact is that the best political sleuths in the country have tried, for four long years, to get something big on Hopkins and his administration. Their researches have netted exactly nothing. As a result it has slowly dawned on Washington that Hopkins is doing a colossal job almost miraculouly well and both the organization and the man have risen rapidly, of late, in the esteem of the sharp-eyed gentlemen of both parties on Capitol Hill.

Hopkins was a relief administrator before he took over in Washington. Mr. Roosevelt, in 1931, picked him to run the New York State emergency relief administration. Before that he had been a New York City social worker—of the Frances Perkins, Lillian Wald, Bob Wagner, Eleanor Roosevelt school. When he came to Washington, therefore, he knew what it was all about. The scale was larger but the idea was the same.

Hopkins' Washington success, however, is not entirely due to his familiarity with the problem. He has other qualifications. He is cynical, caustic, and excessively direct. Those qualities got him in bad with the politicians. That failed to bother him, a fact that subsequently helped him with the politicians—who customarily have a great, if prudently concealed, respect for public officials who can't be bothered. And the fact that he says what he thinks even though—as is usually the case—it is bad news, has been an asset to him.

Like many cynics, Hopkins is a sentimentalist. His mouth is a bit twisted. But his eyes give him away. I do not recall that he was ever maudlin about the millions of out-of-work Americans in his charge. And he dislikes paternalism. But I am sure that he has a feeling of personal responsibility toward them. Some of them have gone a bit hay-wire. But the frequency with which he is forced to administer hard-boiled medicine to the lunatic fringe has not altered his belief in the decency, the industry, and the Americanism of the overwhelming majority of the millions who are carried on his rolls. That is a further reason why he does his job so well.

Moreover, he has assembled a remarkable administrative personnel. Washington, since the New Deal, has witnessed the coming and going of a good many strangely assorted organizations. From the standpoint of a city that makes all of its judgments by political standards, the personnel of the WPA probably ranks with the strangest of them. The WPA offices in the Johnson-Walker building and the overflow quarters in the Washington auditorium are filled with young men and women in whom the fires of the early crusading days of the New Deal still burn as brightly as ever. The crusade has become somewhat routine. Files and reports and questionnaires and the earthy business of bookkeeping have somewhat cut off the earlier view of far horizons. But get a WPA executive away from his three phones, his six buzzers and his arriving and departing telegrams and it is soon evident that the old "make America over" spirit is still there.

Most of the members of this crusading force are exceedingly able. Most of them work for the WPA, not because they could not get a job anywhere else, but because they like it. Some of them do not need to work at all. Dallas Dort—who is the acting director of projects—dropped in on the organization a week after returning from a world cruise. He knew Corrington Gill, one of Hopkins' Assistant Administrators and wanted to have a look at the organization. Gill, at the time, was putting together the first CWA machinery. Dort promised to stay on for two weeks and help him. He has been there ever since. He is twenty-nine years old; a Princeton A.B., with a law degree from the University of Michigan.

David Weintraub is the chief WPA statistician. He is thirty-three, a graduate of the College of the City of New York; M.A. at Columbia, with two further years of graduate study to his credit. He was, for a time, the white-haired statistician at the National Bureau of Economic Research. His statistical work at the WPA has been monumental. At times he has had as many as 1200 assistants working with him. The government long before Weintraub's arrival or the advent of the New Deal had collected in its various departments probably the best aggregation of statisticians in the United States. It is generally agreed that Weintraub ranks with the top half dozen.

The WPA Director of Finance—paymaster—is David A. Holmes. Holmes is thirty-two—a graduate of the University of Syracuse. He was formerly connected with the Dictaphone Sales Corporation. The Director of Reports is Emerson Ross. Ross is also thirty-two. He is a graduate of Dartmouth and of the Tuck School of Business. He was formerly in research work with the Metropolitan Life Insurance Company and then went to the Reconstruction Finance Corporation as a statistician.

Those men are a fair example of the second-string WPA executives. They are not bureaucrats. They do not expect to stay, permanently, with the government. They look upon the WPA as a big job and they have imagination enough to want to have a part in it—even though, financially, they can barely manage to scrape along in Washington. They are not Democrats or Republicans or Socialists. They are free lance liberals. They are for Mr. Roosevelt because his program, at present, seems to be the liberal program. They would be against him if it were not.

Farther down in the scale—through the regional, state, and district offices there is, naturally, somewhat less ability than at the top. Nevertheless, the men at the top have set the standards for the selection of those at the lower levels and on those levels a remarkably high percentage of the personnel is made up of similarly able and socially-minded young people.

The organization—being filled with individualists—is highly temperamental. It is the force of Hopkins' personality that hold them together. One of his top assistants once remarked to me:

"Most of us here at WPA wouldn't cross the street on the orders of WPA. But on an order from Hopkins—if he signed it himself—we'd all with one accord jump out of this seventh-story window."

The young men in Mr. Wallace's Department of Agriculture have the same evangelical feeling about their chief. But I should say that there are fewer prima donnas among the men at Agriculture than at WPA. Hopkins has a prima donna in almost every cubbyhole. It is quite likely that if his influence were to be withdrawn, his smooth-running organization, overnight, would become a shambles.

Meanwhile, the organization continues to be smooth-running and that is a further reason why the job committed to it and to Hopkins has been so well done.

In point of view and temperament, Hopkins more closely resembles the President than any important administration executive. I think that Mr. Roosevelt is inclined to regard Harry as one of his boys. But there is, none-the-less, a deep bond between them. Unlike the relationship between the President and Mr. Morgenthau, the Secretary of the Treasury, Harry's status with Mr. Roosevelt is not due to social propinquity but to intellectual understanding.

Both the President and Mr. Hopkins like to think "in the large" and they both enjoy action on the grand scale. Both of them are stubborn. Both love a fight. They both enjoy brilliant people, but not profound ones. Harry is less affable and occasionally likes solitude. But, like the President, he is essentially gregarious. Like Mr. Roosevelt, too, Harry believes that the government can make the world a better place to live in and he, too, is inclined to be evangelical about it.

Hopkins, however, is not and never has been a practical politician. If he had not been given his great crusading chance by a man who is a very practical politician, he would probably have gone on through life nursing his dreams in relative obscurity. When he first came to Washington, he was not only indifferent to politics and politicians, he was generally impatient with them. More recently, however, his manner has been observed to have undergone a considerable change. Toward the leaders on Capitol Hill he has shown signs of something amounting almost to deference. He has begun, on a small scale, to seek out and privately to cultivate some of the more important among them—"the key men," as Washington puts it. Both the key men and Hopkins have apparently enjoyed the experience. At

any rate, by midsummer of 1937 he had come to occupy as high a place in the regard of Congress as any
of the New Deal chiefs. And there were reports that a
few men on the Hill, looking toward 1940, were already Hopkins men.

No one would gather from Hopkins that his thoughts
are running on ahead to the next Presidential year—
any more than one can gather that from any of the
men whose thoughts, none-the-less, are running that
way. Privately, he expresses himself as entirely fed up
with Washington and anxious to get into more lucrative pursuits. Presidential urging and the promise that
when Congress creates a new Cabinet post Hopkins will
get it, have kept him at his job.

But if Hopkins—strolling from his office past the
State, War and Navy Buildings to the entrance to the
White House—granting interviews to the press, reading them on the front page of the next day's papers,
sitting in consultation with Congressional leaders or
finding himself across from the President in the oval
room at the White House with a voice in Mr. Roosevelt's most important decisions—does not think long
thoughts about himself, he is, I should say, almost
unique among first-rank New Deal administrators. And
if he is not thinking such thoughts for himself he has
plenty of assistants who are thinking them for him.

Meanwhile, there is no doubt whatever that the
WPA organization, itself, has political potentialities

large enough to make a machine politician's mouth water. If the WPA is not in politics, it is not because the actual WPA set-up and the nature of the undertakings it sponsors are not of a sort to be politically useful. In fact, no other mechanism, in the whole vast list of New Deal mechanism, could be so quickly converted into a political machine. Harry Hopkins did not plan it that way. Any administrator, with his kind of a job, would have had to set up his kind of an organization. Nevertheless, in the impending show-down between the New Deal and the old-line Democratic organization, Harry Hopkins' vast WPA mechanism is sure to be crucially important.

It is just possible that it may be important enough to make the man who heads it the New Deal candidate in 1940. If—as substantial evidence indicates—Mr. Roosevelt proposes not only to break with but, finally, to break up the old national machinery of the Democratic party, take over what is worth salvaging and put together an entirely bona fide New Deal party, he could find no candidate more to his own liking than Mr. Hopkins. Meanwhile, it is worth observing that Harry Hopkins, since the second inauguration, has joined the little group of White House intimates and his name, more often than that of any Cabinet member, appears in the list of those who are included in the President's informal and, therefore, more important conferences. And, whatever Mr. Roosevelt's 1940 aims

may be, it is not to be lightly dismissed that Harry
Hopkins would probably be Mrs. Roosevelt's candidate.

In mid April 1937, Mr. Hopkins' report to Congress indicated that 2,085,000 workers were employed
on WPA projects. An additional 600,000 young people
were being aided through the National Youth Administration—a WPA subsidiary. For the year ending June
30, 1938, Mr. Hopkins—after a hard fight that saw
such administration stalwarts as the late Senator Robinson and Senator Jimmy Byrnes of North Carolina in
the opposition—secured from Congress the sum he
asked for: $1,500,000,000.

The organization through which this vast sum is administered leads up to Harry Hopkins' ninth floor office in the Walker-Johnson Building. But it reaches
down and out from his office into almost every community in America. The administrative staff has more
than 30,000 people on it. The staff is organized on five
levels: national, regional, state, district, and local. From
a considerable amount of personal observation, I should
say that this administrative army of 30,000 has fewer
lame ducks and superannuates in it than any organization which the government of the United States has
sponsored in a good many decades. In the matter of
political experience, a good many of them are novices.
In the matter of brains, most of them outclass the men
who run the country's local political machines.

Next to Harry Hopkins, at the top of the organization, is Aubrey Williams, Deputy Administrator of the WPA and Director of the National Youth Administration. Williams is an Alabaman. His grandfather was a rich planter whose fortune was wiped out in the Civil War. His father, trained for leisure, was obliged to work at whatever offered. He became a blacksmith. At six, Aubrey Williams went to work in a torpedo factory; at seven he was running errands for a Birmingham department store. His family's cash income, at times, did not exceed $3.50 a week. Aubrey went to night school, worked his way through college, got into the war, stayed on in France after the Armistice and returned to the United States with a doctorate of philosophy from the University of Bordeaux. Before coming to stand at Harry Hopkins' right hand, he was engaged in social work in Ohio and Wisconsin.

Williams is tall, unassuming, serious about his job but not too serious about other matters. He is an able administrator. He has spent the millions allotted to him for the youth of the country with very little audible grinding of organizational gears. He makes it a point to steer clear of the politicians, and to keep close to Mrs. Roosevelt—who has a very active interest in the NYA. Like Hopkins, Williams is a crusader, who has seen enough of the world to have his zeal tempered with a measure of cynicism.

Probably the most influential person in the WPA set-up, next to Hopkins and Williams, is Mrs. Ellen

Woodward. Mrs. Woodward is a Mississippian and a former member of the Mississippi state legislature. She is moderately young, attractive, extremely energetic, with a mind that takes in everything that is going on, and an inclination never to hesitate to say what she thinks about it. Hopkins, and a good many other of his assistant executives, have a great deal of respect for what she thinks and those who may not like it are impelled, because of the influence she wields, to give an attentive ear. Technically, Mrs. Woodward is in charge of all white collar and women's projects. Actually, she is confined to no such pigeonhole.

There are three other top executives in the Washington office. F. C. Harrington is assistant administrator in charge of engineering. Corrington Gill is assistant administrator in charge of Finance, economic research, and planning. David K. Niles is assistant administrator in charge of labor relations and the general information service.

Gill is a streamlined executive if there ever was one. He is nervous, wiry, affable—the kind of administrator who does several things simultaneously without getting the wires crossed. He is a graduate of the University of Wisconsin, was formerly with the Federal Employment Stabilization Board and before that was a financial correspondent, in Washington, for a string of newspapers. He is well under forty. He works with figures and his office goes in for charts and graphs. But

he has a mind for economic trends and the long look.
Like all of Hopkins' top associates he regards the WPA
not merely as an emergency job, but as a sign of the
times. Also like most of Hopkins' associates, Gill stays
with the WPA, not because he could not make more
money elsewhere, but because of his loyalty to Hopkins
and—more important—his belief that the New Deal is
making the kind of history he wants to have a hand in
making.

Niles, who is in charge of labor relations and information, is not streamlined. He is bald, a little rotund,
wears thick glasses, works hard but never hurries, and
gives the impression that he is naïve and otherworldly—
which he decidedly is not. Niles is from Boston. He
knows Massachusetts politics—a fact which leaves him
very little to learn. He is one of that state's seasoned
liberals. For many years he was associated with the
Ford Hall Forum. In 1924 he had charge of the Massachusetts end of the La Follette-Wheeler campaign.
In 1932 he resurrected his La Follette Progressive organization and put it effectively in the field on behalf
of Mr. Roosevelt. He had a good deal to do on a national scale with the Progressives-for-Roosevelt movement in 1936. But, even in that year, Massachusetts
was his special vineyard.

He is close to James Roosevelt, has the ear of the
President, and is one of the little group of contrivers
who meet—late at night—with Tom Corcoran and

Ben Cohen to appraise the current state of the nation
and determine what can be done about it. He is Harry
Hopkins' political ear-to-the-ground. If a Hopkins'
Presidential boom is on the way, it is safe to say that
Dave Niles not only knows about it, but that he was
the person who called the meeting at which it started.

I am sure that Niles cares little or nothing about the
Democratic Party. But he cares a great deal about the
so-called liberal movement. He is for Mr. Roosevelt.
But he would like to see a bona fide liberal party. Politically, I think he is much more at home at the headquarters of the Labor-Nonpartisan League in the Willard Hotel than in the offices of the Democratic National
Committee in the National Press Building.

For administrative purposes, the WPA has divided
the country into five regions. Each regional director is
appointed by Hopkins, reports to Hopkins and has,
under him, a staff modeled exactly on the pattern of
the Washington organization. Each one of the 48 states
also has a state organization, similarly organized. Each
state director is likewise appointed by Hopkins and answerable to him. The regional directors are in constant
contact with Washington and it is their business to keep
a check on state activities and to interpret the WPA to
the state organizations.

Each state, in turn, is broken down into districts, presided over by a district director. The district director's
set-up has all the items in it which are found in the

state, regional, and national offices. He has a director of
finance, a director of engineering, and an information
service and staffs for each. His appointment comes with
Hopkins' O.K., but he makes his reports to the state
director. There are some 350 such district organizations
in the nation. The district organization has direct contact with the localities and the specific projects being
carried on in them. As I have already pointed out, the
entire organization—from the local administrator and
his staff up through the district, the state, the region
and including the national officers—has more than 30,-
000 people in it.

It is possible to get something of an idea of the vast
scope of the work which this organization carries on
from the fact that—in the early summer of 1937—the
WPA had more than 170,000 projects actually under
way. Fifty thousand more had been approved.

But there is more to the WPA than size. There is
quality. In fact, the scope of this organization (30,000
people, employing more than 2,000,000 workers on
170,000 different undertakings) is no more significant
than the nature of the projects.

In terms of improvements in the nation's physical
plant, the record of the WPA is beyond anything that
the Federal government—in any like period—ever
achieved. It has built 29,000 miles of new roads and
improved 94,000 miles of existing roads—constructing,
in the process, 7600 new bridges, reconditioning 13,000

old bridges, building 86,000 culverts and repairing 27,-000 others.

By September 15, 1936, the WPA had improved or repaired 7200 school buildings and built 1100 new schools—from one-room rural size to city schools housing a thousand or more pupils. It had improved, repaired or built new thousands of other public buildings: hospitals, fire-houses, recreational buildings. It had constructed 3000 athletic fields and playgrounds, 1500 parks and fairgrounds, 95 golf courses and had built or improved 300 swimming pools. It had made 45 new aviation landing fields and improved 67 others; built 4450 miles of trunk and lateral sewers and 130,000 miles of service connections and laid 2400 miles of water mains.

These, of course, were mostly large-scale operations. The number of smaller, less dramatic undertakings is even greater. On September 15, 1936, for example, 10,052 sewing rooms were in operation for WPA women. These rooms, up to that date, had produced 60,839,800 articles—mostly clothes. In the library section, more than 11,142,000 books had been repaired. In conservation work, 967,000 acres had been drained to eradicate plant disease, 528,000 acres drained to eradicate mosquitoes, 3,720,000 gallons of spray had been used on threatened trees. The WPA had likewise served 72,000,000 school lunches, made 9,110,000 medical, dental or nursing visits to homes, had canned

6316 tons of food and run 8987 home gardens. In addition to these things, it has provided millions of free music lessons, organized scores of symphony and community orchestras, made WPA bands a commonplace, staged hundreds of plays under the Federal Theatre Project, prepared traveler's guides to interesting American tourist centers, taught hundreds of thousands of adults to read and write, directed playground and recreational activities in a great many communities, large and small, and done a vast number of needful odd-jobs throughout the nation.

The WPA is unique in American history in the number of people it supports. It is just as unique in the vast assortment of projects on which it employs them while they are supported. There is, I think, no doubt whatever that work relief adapted, as WPA work relief is adapted, to the capacity or skill of the individual worker has maintained both the employability and the morale of the individual employed. This is so much the case that in many large cities—such as New York—the WPA relief rolls have become the Social Register among the unemployed. Its executives —having definite jobs in mind—want only the best and they sort around among the available out-of-job workers until they get them.

It was primarily to maintain the morale of the unemployed that America's unemployment problem was handled on the WPA plan. The WPA must get a major share of the credit for having brought millions of Americans through the last years of the depression without serious impairment of their employability. But it is the success of the WPA in doing the job assigned to it that accounts, in large part, for its political potentialities.

It can hardly be questioned, I think, that there is an already considerable and steadily developing class consciousness among WPA workers. They do not—thanks to the program of work relief—regard themselves as "reliefers." And they are not reliefers. They have been spared the depressing effect of the dole. They have had to work for their money. They can point to definite and important things that they have done. Most of them would probably take jobs in private industry if permanent jobs, at living wages, came along. But in the meantime they do not, in any sense, regard themselves as charity cases. They believe that they have a right to what they are getting. They propose to do all that they can do to make certain that they will continue to get it.

Up to the present they have only begun to get together in a definite organization. The Workers' Alliance is, I believe, the only national organization of the unemployed. The WA is decidedly left-wing, farther to the left, by a good deal, than the much railed against CIO. It has an aggressive set-up in almost every city in the country. Every important relief executive has had to meet its delegations, endure its picketing, and watch its parades. Its paid-up membership may include 3 per-cent of all the two million WPA unemployed. In larger cities like New York where it claims to have 110 locals, it is a factor of considerable importance. Elsewhere, it is less significant.

But the Workers' Alliance undoubtedly speaks for a great many more of the unemployed than it has signed up. By no means all of those for whom it speaks have any Communistic leanings—unless the belief that jobs for the unemployed is a government responsibility is Communistic. But a great many of them are becoming class-minded. They are beginning to know their way around politically. They are learning, also, how to be politically articulate. They know who the local political bosses are, where they hang out and how to speak up in their presence. They are learning the names of their rep-resentatives in Congress and how to address their letters of complaint and demand. More than ever before in their lives, they make it a point to vote and the way they vote is determined, not by the machine politicians, but by the relief question and the attitude of the various candidates on that they are and increasingly will be a definite political bloc—large enough to be a factor in any national election and a decisive factor in some.

Harry Hopkins and his administrators throughout the country have not deliberately fostered the growth of such a bloc. They have not appealed to the unem-ployed to organize and get into politics. But it is quite likely that they welcome the development. As I have already indicated, the WPA, to a large majority of the men who run it, is a cause. They not only believe in what the WPA is concretely accomplishing. They believe, with zeal, in the people for whom it is accomplishing it and in their right to a larger share in the economic good things of life. Providing that larger share is what they regard as liberalism. And, with varying leanings from the middle-of-the-road to the left, almost all of them are liberals.

They would say, I think, that next to organized labor the workers on the rolls of the WPA are the most important constituent for the making of an authentic liberal political movement in the United States. Most of the men and women at or near the top would never stay in the organization if the dispensing of relief appeared to them to be the sum total of the WPA's significance. I am sure that a good many of them stay on because they see—or think that they see—a force emerging out of the WPA that can, if properly led, have a permanently liberalizing effect upon America's political and economic life.

I think it would be going too far to say that the executives of the WPA are unaware of the present political possibilities in their organization. As I have previously pointed out, the propaganda of the WPA was exceedingly useful during the last campaign. Such WPA films as "A Better Indiana," "A Better Ohio," "A Bet-

ter Illinois," "A Better Pennsylvania," widely circulated in the respective states, are bound to be of a very
definite political value even though, directly, there is
no politics in them. The all-Negro WPA film, "We
Work Again," is a good picture, but it is also good
politics. It is a direct stimulus to the development of a
self-conscious Negro bloc—independent of parties and
discriminating on issues.

The information service—which put out more than
400 releases during 1936—had full-time publicity directors in every state and sixty such directors in various
district offices. It, likewise, is a political asset. I am told
that during the last campaign the only two states which
did not go down the line selling the WPA were Maine
and Vermont. It is said, also, that the only pre-election
forecast whose accuracy equaled that of Jim Farley was
one prepared by Harry Hopkins from data furnished
him by his state offices and submitted to the President
a few days before the election. It was, at least, an indication of a sincere desire to help toward such a conclu-
sive triumph that the WPA—during the last campaign
—supplied to every Democratic Senator and Representative a completely tabulated list of WPA projects in his
state, with the money spent, the number of people employed, and the nature of the projects all conveniently
listed.

All this does not prove that the WPA is dominated
by political considerations. But it is true that, in any

major political show-down in the United States in the near future, the WPA organization and the increasing political sensitiveness of two million WPA people will have to be reckoned with. In its business of work-relief, the WPA has done an enormous job extraordinarily well. But in the incidental and, perhaps, inevitable business of putting back of the present administration the kind of support which is likely to make the New Deal self-perpetuating it has—for good or ill—a major political achievement to its credit.

CHAPTER VII

THE FARMERS' ONE BIG UNION

I THINK it is true that Mr. Roosevelt—next to carrying Pennsylvania and his home town of Hyde Park—was more pleased at his victory in Kansas than in any other incidental election triumph. He wanted to carry Kansas because it was Governor Landon's home state. But he also wanted to carry it because Kansas is something of a symbol of the agricultural West. Like most of that country, it is normally Republican. In fact, its Republicanism is considerably more rock-ribbed than that of near-by states. A victory in Kansas, therefore, was the ultimate evidence of the approval of the nation's farmers for the policies of the New Deal.

But the farmers of Kansas—even though their traditional Republicanism goes back to the Civil War—are not essentially different from farmers anywhere else in the nation. They are traders. They recognize a good thing when they see it. Ever since 1921, when the depression first hit the farms of America, they had listened to the promises of successive administrations and witnessed, to their sorrow, the collapse of successive farm policies. It was not particularly novel when Mr. Roosevelt, in 1932, promised to do something for the farmers. It was decidedly novel, however, when what he did actually worked and the farmers, by 1936, found themselves well out of the depression. Their sentiments may have been wrenched a bit when they voted the Democratic ticket. But, being more practical than sentimental, they voted it.

Between 1932 and 1935 the cash income of the nation's farmers increased 81 percent. Some of that cash came from the Federal government, under payments of the Triple A. Some of it came from increased farm prices. But whatever the source of the money there was no doubt in the agricultural mind in 1936 as to the source of the benefits.

It should be pointed out, however, that the farm program of the First New Deal did not reach to and include all of the farmers of the country. The Triple A was, in general, an upper-class farm program. There are some nine million farm families in the United States. The New Deal has made its most significant contributions to the economic well-being of the upper three million. It has yet to reach down in the economic scale and do something for the lower three million—particularly the tenant farmers, the share-croppers, and that considerable farm population which is endeavoring to live on worn-out or eroded land. Their problems are likely to be included in the agricultural objectives of the Second New Deal. At any rate—and much to the surprise of the Department of Agriculture—Congress, in its 1937 session, substantially increased the appropriations which had been requested for the Resettlement Administration.

Meanwhile, the New Deal's economic aid to agriculture has considerable political significance. Not only the money given to the farmers, but also the process by which the giving has been administered have greatly increased the political articulation of America's farm voters and, beyond that, has begun the development of an actual political solidarity among them. They have broken with their political traditions and, for the first time on so widespread a scale, they are ready to vote for the party that offers them the most and that appears most likely to make good on its promises. It might be difficult to swing a majority of them to a third party in 1940. But if the Republican leadership undergoes no bona fide metamorphosis and if the conservative Democrats should wrest control of the party machine away from Mr. Roosevelt and the New Dealers then—having already tasted the benefits of political independence —it is possible that a large bloc of them might make common cause with labor against both the old party organizations.

The important point is that the machinery for farm

solidarity—for the farmers' one big union—has already been created. The story of its creation begins in the Department of Agriculture. It begins with Henry Wallace and his young men.

The Wallace Brain Trust is probably the ablest in Washington. On the administrative and personal side it is headed by Paul Appleby, Administrative Assistant to the Secretary, a native Missourian, a graduate of Grinnell College in Iowa, owner now of several country newspapers. Appleby sits just outside the Secretary's door, takes off his hands a multitude of administrative details, is affable to all comers and divides his evenings between heavy reading and heavy conversation. He can say what he thinks to the Secretary and does—generally to the Secretary's benefit. Next in line is James D. LeCron—politically astute and almost as close to Wallace as Appleby. A little more remote, but still well within the Brain Trust circle, are Louis Bean and Mordecai Ezekial, both economists. Bean is a native of Lithuania, and a postgraduate of Harvard. He was in the Department of Agriculture before the present administration, but it was Mr. Wallace who rescued him from Civil Service obscurity and put him where his information would be within reach. Mordecai Ezekial, since he has ideas and makes speeches about them, has been one of the lesser thorns in the side of the New Deal and of Mr. Wallace. He is a Virginian, eligible to membership in the First Families of Virginia, and a graduate of the

University of Maryland. Both officially and unofficially Ezekial is economic adviser to the Secretary. Paul Appleby and LeCron probably have more influence on Mr. Wallace's thinking and the way on which he makes up his mind on matters both in and outside of Agriculture than any other individuals. How the Secretary expresses what he thinks is a problem for Jack Fleming—a Cornell graduate and a newspaper man who has a desk in the information section of the Department and almost always is one of the men called in when the Secretary has a speech to make—which, of late, has been rather frequently.

The important fact about these men is not that they make up a Brain Trust. Washington is full of Brain Trusts. But the Wallace Brain Trust is distinguished because it is more intelligent than most, it has more definite objectives and, in Mr. Wallace and his agricultural program, it has better material with which to work. If its members share an ambition about Mr. Wallace which he does not publicly acknowledge, they share with him those long-time ideas about farm solidarity which, if they continue to bear fruit, are likely to bring that ambition within reach.

Of course, this devoted effort may not put Henry Wallace in the White House. It is an axiom of American politics that booms which bloom early are subject to frost. But if this boom withers, if in 1940 Mr. Roosevelt's hands are laid on some other head, it will not be because Mr. Wallace has faltered in his understanding and practice of the New Deal gospel or has failed, in his special field, to do a job of almost Presidential proportions. No other Department of the government is so deeply indoctrinated, as Agriculture, with New Deal ideas or has so faithfully sought to make those ideas work. No previous Secretary of Agriculture has been able to devise a farm program substantial enough to constitute the first planks in a Presidential platform. And what, in the end, may turn out to be even more important, Mr. Wallace, with his gospel and his program, has got the farmers of the nation in a state of mind and of organization that makes them more potent politically than they have been at any time since the Populist uprising of the 'nineties.

America's farm population is approximately 32,000,-000. America's farmers, like farmers everywhere, are practical, independent, and fundamentally conservative. With an eight billion dollar cash income in 1936 they run the nation's largest business. What happens to that business is a national problem. But the farmers, in the past, have seldom thought nationally and they have had practically no national solidarity. They have been sectional in their thinking and, as a result, their economic aches and pains have almost always had only sectional treatment.

This disunity, although it may have had its source in the traditional provincialism of an agricultural population, was fed and nurtured by politicians. The farmers of the North were Republicans, bag and baggage. The baggage included the Republicans' high tariff and on that the northern farmer, for many years, pinned his hope of prosperity. The farmers of the South were Democrats and free traders. The margin of profit on their cotton crop was fixed in a world market. Whatever the merits of the issue that divided them, it was the business of the politicians to see to it that the division was maintained. Any idea that there might be a common ground between the two positions on which the farmers of the nation could stand together was likely to disrupt the solidly Democratic South or the almost equally solid Republican agricultural North and was nipped before it blossomed.

The story is told in the Department of Agriculture of a young agriculturalist who returned to Washington from a trip through the farming areas excited by his discovery of the fact that the farmers of the nation have a community of interest and consumed with a desire to make them aware of it. Moreover, he had a plan. He proposed excursion trains: farmers of the North shipped at reduced rates and by the car-load into the South to look over southern farm problems and get acquainted with the southern farmer and southern farmers brought north, in quantity, in the same way and for the same purpose. The young man's idea is said to have found some favor in the Department. But when wind of what was stirring reached Capitol Hill those members of Congress whose political lease on life depended upon the farm vote and stood to be jeopardized by any untoward development in the farmers' point of view promptly turned on the pressure and the young man and his idea were suppressed. It was Henry Wallace and his program that finally blew off the lid and, without exactly resorting to the expedient of intersectional excursions, undertook the creation of a farmer class consciousness and a national agricultural solidarity.

In 1933, when Mr. Wallace took over the Department of Agriculture, the time was ripe for such an effort, and Mr. Wallace was very much the man for such a time. He, more than any other member of Mr. Roosevelt's Cabinet and more, even, than Mr. Roosevelt, dreams dreams and sees visions. He might easily have been a poet or an evangelist, more likely a poet. There is hardly enough surface-fire in his make-up for successful evangelism. But there is plenty of mysticism. He is a great believer, not only in the ordinary religious sense, but more particularly in regard to the destiny of society. The New Order is a major article of faith with him and if he has kept close to agriculture and out of those New Order undertakings which were not his responsibility his restraint has been due to his desire to maintain the political amenities and not because he has no long thoughts for anything but farming.

Wallace is probably the most accessible of the New

Deal's Number One administrators. He sees almost
every one. If his own office is occupied he comes out of
it and shakes hands, all around, in the reception room.
I suspect that the Department of Agriculture turns out
more people every day who are able to say "I talked
with the Secretary" than any other government department. It is not easy to know what sort of an impression
the Secretary makes on a critical caller. His press conferences—thanks to his own desire to improve them and
to the intensive coaching of his Young Men—have come
down to earth and are at least as much of a success as
those of most Cabinet members. But unlike Mr. Roosevelt, however cordially he receives you or urges you to
remain beyond your appointed time, he is apt to appear
abstracted. His mind may be on what you have to say
but his eyes have a far-away look in them.

Wallace's great enthusiasm is agriculture and the corn
fields of Iowa are his first love. Mr. Roosevelt, in 1933,
may have seen in him the making of a corn-hog statesman and called him to the Cabinet to provide a wind-
ward anchor among the normally Republican voters of
the agricultural West. Henry Wallace, himself, was a
Republican with a long and distinguished Republican
lineage. In fact, although he broke with the party in
1928, he remained a registered Republican until the
Spring of 1936 when he signed, officially, with the
Democrats. Moreover, there was no doubt that he
knew both the language and the problems of the corn

and hog belt. But when he came to Washington he had more on his mind than corn and hogs. He had the agricultural map of the United States on his mind and the belief that, given half a chance, he could bring the farmers of the nation into their own. I question whether anyone was more astonished than Mr. Roosevelt to discover that his Secretary of Agriculture was to be the New Deal's premier crusader and that out of the Department of Agriculture was to come the New Deal's first crusade.

But he was not left long in doubt about it. On the fifth of March 1933, the President issued his call for a special session of Congress. It had been informally agreed that Congress should convene for three days only, pass the legislation necessary to meet the banking crisis and adjourn. The date for the emergency session was set for March 12th. When this announcement was made Henry Wallace had scarcely had time to unpack his bags. After it was made he never found time to finish unpacking them. If there was to be a crusade this was the moment to start it. He called in Rex Tugwell, his newly appointed Assistant Secretary. Tugwell knew little enough about agriculture. But he knew a good deal about crusades. He agreed with Wallace that the time was ripe. On the eighth of March the two of them met the President after dinner in his second-floor study at the White House. They pored over Wallace's agricultural map of the nation until nearly midnight. By that time the President, too, had agreed. If the farmers could get together on a legislative program he was ready to keep Congress in session long enough to pass it.

Wallace and Tugwell hurried back to the Department, aroused the operator and spent most of the rest of the night in long-distance telephone conversation with as many of the nation's farm leaders as could be routed out of bed. Wallace knew just the men. He knew the arguments and supported by the emergency and a go-ahead from the just-inaugurated President he was confident, when that night's work was finished, that bigger and better things had begun for agriculture.

Two days later he was surer of it than ever. The farm leaders he had consulted, fifty of them, turned up in Washington as he had urged them to do. They came direct from their trains to the Secretary's office. They seldom left it for the next thirty-six hours. They were representative of every major farm interest, north and south. They had never before sat around the same table and few of them were acquainted. But that thirty-six hour session not only laid the basis for the farm legislation incorporated in the Triple A. It made the first significant dent in the walls of agricultural sectionalism and proved to Henry Wallace that the farm solidarity which he had always believed to be desirable had become a possibility.

It was two months before the farm bill was passed by Congress. In that time inter-sectional conferences between farm leaders had become a daily routine in Wallace's office. Wallace reported frequently by radio to the farmers just what was under way. Farm papers, with very few exceptions, loaded their editorial pages with explanations of the proposed measure and with praise for the consult-everybody technique of the new Secretary of Agriculture.

Every day the Secretary's outer offices and the corridors beyond them were filled with increasing crowds of farmers who had come to Washington to see for themselves what it was all about. Most of them left Washington not altogether sure what it was all about, but convinced—with some one of Henry Wallace's able associates doing the convincing—that henceforth farmers were to have the first and last say in the making of farm policies and that, at last, the farmers of the nation were going places.

In this fashion, the farm bill was sold to the farmers as their bill. And in the process of making it their bill and selling it, Wallace brought about what was probably the most effective and certainly the most genuinely national mobilization of farm sentiment in the history of American agriculture.

But that was only the beginning. The farmers not only were brought together and given a hand in preparing the Triple A legislation; but once passed, the question of their coöperation in it was put directly up to them. Undoubtedly, with cash payments in the offing, the dice were heavily loaded in favor of the administration's program in the various referenda which were held on it. During 1934 and 1935, more than four million votes were cast on the question of crop curtailment by wheat, cotton, tobacco, and corn and hog farmers. Of this number 3,700,000 voted for continuance of the program. But the important, long-time fact was the voting, itself, and not the size of the vote. The farmers were not only being singled out for special attention, they were being asked to speak their minds, by ballot, on the kind of special attention they were getting. Never before had class consciousness, in any group, been given a more effective stimulant.

But that, too, was more or less a preliminary achievement. It is chiefly in the administration of the program that the Wallace dream of farm solidarity has been given form and substance. Under the Triple A the farmers have been and are their own administrators and in the process of administering there has been created what is, as Mr. Wallace calls it, "a hierarchy"—a farm organization that reaches directly from his desk in the Department of Agriculture down to 75 percent of the farmers and the last rural township in the nation. The government of the United States has never before stood sponsor for anything like this either in agriculture or anywhere else.

What it amounts to is that in exactly four years the farmers of the United States have been brought together

[163]

into One Big Union which, if it has not entirely destroyed their sectionalism, has established the foundations for a farm solidarity which is all the more significant because it is based on self-interest and is producing dividends. They have learned that they can get together and that getting together pays. The result of what they have learned may not change the pattern of our political and economic life. But it will certainly subject it to a new and uncertain influence.

It was inevitable, of course, that the administration of the crop curtailment phases of the Triple A should be turned over to the farmers. There was no other practical way in which they could be administered. That part of the program, when it got down to the farmer who had signed a contract, required a classification of his farm, an estimate of his acreage, and a regular and accurate account of his production all to the end that the government would know, before sending out its check, that the terms of his contract had been fulfilled. This was a major policing job—one of the largest policing jobs ever undertaken. To have undertaken it with an imported army of government agents would have aroused a resentment among the farmers which even the forthcoming payments would probably not have restrained. Moreover, government agents, even though they were experts, could not possibly know and, short of a considerable period of investigation, could not possibly find out as much about the farms and the farmers of the average rural county as the farmers of that county themselves.

The farmers, therefore, were enlisted to do their own policing and—in enlisting them—there came into being what the Department of Agriculture first called "Production Control Committees" and now calls "Agricultural Conservation Associations" and what Henry Wallace refers to as "economic democracy."

These organizations are established and functioning in every rural township in the United States. Every farmer who signs a contract with the government becomes, automatically, a member. Once every year all the participating farmers of the immediate district, usually of the township, elect from their own number a chairman and two other persons to serve as the local Board of Directors. The chairmen of all the local boards, in turn, constitute the County Committee. The County Committee elects, from its membership, an executive committee of three, one of whom is chosen county chairman. The government pays the members of the local committees on a per diem basis, generally $4.50 a day with no allowance for travel. The county officers receive the same daily pay with a small travel allowance. The post, in other words, is a desirable one.

Between the township and county officers are the government's local administrators. The County Committee sets up an office, generally in the county seat, employs clerical help and keeps the records. Working through the local committees, the county board of directors fixes the details of the contract to be drawn with the individual farmer, determines whether or not the terms of the contract have been fulfilled and, finally, establishes the size of the check which the individual farmer receives. For the year 1937 more than $400,-000,000 was passed on by these committees in benefit payments to farmers.

One step up in this agricultural hierarchy are the state committees. The members of these committees are not elected. They are appointed by the Secretary of Agriculture. Usually, however, they are operating farmers, almost always chosen from the state in which they serve. They maintain a general supervision over the work of the county committees, iron out problems of local administration and serve as interpreters-at-large for the Department to the farmer and of the farmer to the Department. The states, themselves, are grouped in six administrative regions over each of which there is a regional director, appointed by the Secretary of Agriculture and with offices in Washington. The regional director is the liaison between Washington and the state and local committees. The regional directors are answerable to H. R. Tolley, administrator of the Triple A, and Mr. Tolley gets his orders from Henry Wallace.

It is impossible to give the exact number of local and county committees. No one in the Department of Agriculture seems to know. It is known, however, that every rural county in the country is organized and there are 2800 such counties. Last year in the north-central, corn-hog region, 75 percent of the farmers, more than a million and a half of them in number, participated in the government's program and as a result were included in the membership of the local organizations. For the country as a whole, the membership probably averages nearly 70 percent of all the operating farmers of the nation.

This vast machinery, as I have pointed out, was created and is maintained for purposes of administration. But its significance is much more than administrative. It is doing far more for and to the farmers of America than its ostensible business of accounting and disbursing.

Mr. Wallace has told of an official of the Russian government who stopped in at the Department of Agriculture during the early, hectic period that followed the passage of the 1933 farm bill. He was taken through the Department and finally to a vast room, half a city block in area where an army of fifteen hundred clerks, flanked by batteries of comptometers and check-writing machines was turning out 80,000 crop curtailment checks every twenty-four hours. The Russian surveyed the scene with an experienced eye: "Ah," he said, "the revolution!"

He was probably right. There is a revolution in agriculture. But the place to look for it is not in Washington where the checks are mailed but on the farms where they are received. And there is nothing necessarily revolutionary in the checks, themselves. They are only tokens of the fact that the first stage of the revolution has been a success.

Mr. Wallace and his associates would undoubtedly be the first to admit that the check-dispensing activities of this agricultural hierarchy are no adequate measure of its long-time importance. In fact, Mr. Wallace has referred to the county associations as "a genuine revival of the old New England town meeting idea." He has described how they have "reawakened the country-side to the possibilities of economic self-government and to the potentialities of the democratic process." He has said that "in the long run, it may turn out that the greatest benefit of the adjustment programs may be, not the price increase or the benefit checks, but the knowledge among farmers themselves that individual and group interest can be made to coincide, and that the method employed is none other than that of a working, effective democracy."

In other words, this government-sponsored organization has become—as it was bound to be—the farmers' one big union. The local and county committee members are much more than administrators. They are educators and propagandists and—since their posts are elective—some of them, inevitably, are politicians. Their offices have begun to displace the corner-store and the Grange hall as the meeting place for farmers.

It is the responsibility of these local and county officials, not only to apply the policies of the Department of Agriculture, but to explain and sell them. That means frequent township and county meetings. The Department of Agriculture has five thousand extension agents and fifteen hundred home demonstration agents in the field. Increasingly, the itineraries of these agents are arranged in coöperation with the local associations. The technique at all these gatherings is that of open discussion. The farmers are urged to speak their minds. After four years of urging they speak them with increasing frankness and on an increasingly wide range of subjects, some of them a long distance removed from the administrative problems of the Triple A. Their confidence has grown with experience and their education in current economics and politics has kept pace with their self-assurance. A veteran of several administrations in the Department of Agriculture, just returned from a round of such meetings, told me that in his judgment the average agricultural county to-day "has more informed and outspoken farmers in it than five years ago could have been found in three average states."

This process of education, indoctrination and class-action is not merely local in scope. The regional directors, whose offices are in Washington near the top of the hierarchy, are Wallace men. They share his convictions about farm solidarity and their programs reflect that belief. There are regular regional conferences which include in their membership representative farmers from the states of the regional group. But more than regional matters are discussed. The picture that is presented by the officials of the Department is a national picture, and the farmers are left in no doubt about the fact that theirs is a national problem and that its solution requires national unity of action.

At the recent spring meeting of the Northeastern Region, the New England states, the guest of honor was an Indiana farmer, Peter Lux, by name, who was brought on to make a speech as proof of the fact that such national unity is on the way. Many of the dairy-men, potato-, tobacco- and fruit-growers present had never before seen an Indiana farmer. But he stole the show. Henry Wallace, speaking at this same gathering, and evidently taking his cue from the demonstration for Peter Lux, declared that the best way to insure America's economic future is "to have the farmers organize and get their fair share of the Federal power."

It is because such exhilarating doctrine is preached in season and out by spokesmen for the government and supported, year after year, by substantial payments from the Federal Treasury that the local and county associations although they continue to serve an administrative purpose, have long since become, as Mr. Wallace describes them, ventures in "economic democracy." They are—as they are encouraged to be—the means by which the farmers of the nation are being trained in the thinking and the practice of solidarity and the channel through which they are being urged to make their bid for political and economic power. Whatever happens to the Triple A, the New Deal, or Mr. Wallace, no one who has had any first hand contact with these associations believes for a minute that the farmers will ever surrender them.

But their contribution toward farm solidarity and class consciousness, however adequate it may appear to be, is significantly supplemented by another government-sponsored project. In forty-one states, the Department of Agriculture has established Farmers' Discussion Groups for the free and unhampered exchange of opinions on current problems of economics and politics. In some thirty-five states, these groups are extensively organized. At the present time probably 80,000 of them are in actual operation.

Here, too, there is something of a hierarchy. Actual maintenance and extension of this project are in the hands of four regional directors, who, in turn, appoint state leaders. It is the business of the state leader to find local leaders, get local units established and keep them going. The local units meet, on an average, sixteen times during the year. During the past winter nearly two million farmers participated in their discussions.

At the head of this organization is Carl Taeusch. Taeusch is a doctor of philosophy. In fact, he taught philosophy, for a time, in the graduate school of the University of Chicago, and M. L. Wilson, the present

Undersecretary of Agriculture, was one of his pupils. Taeusch was teaching in the Harvard School of Business Administration when the idea for these discussion groups was born. M. L. Wilson got in touch with him and—already convinced that the atmosphere at the Harvard School was not particularly congenial—he accepted with alacrity. He is a man to Wallace's liking: relatively young, a good executive, and, more important, possessed of an active imagination and a zeal to leave his mark upon the social order. He is as quiet and unassuming as Wallace, and like him inclined to dream. Like many young executives in the New Deal he smokes a pipe. Between attempts to keep it lighted he explained to me how the farmers' appetite for these local forums was growing so fast that his facilities for training leaders had been entirely outgrown. He was particularly impressed by the fact that this growth seemed to be most rapid in certain states of the South—Virginia, South Carolina and Arkansas in particular.

"This," he said, "is the beginning of the end of southern agricultural peasantry."

The Department of Agriculture, through Taeusch's organization, supplies discussion materials in the form of pamphlets illustrated with charts, maps, and pictures, and generously filled with provocative questions and illustrative material. Among the subjects discussed in the current season were these: "What Should Be the Farmers' Share in the National Income?"; "Should Farm

Ownership Be a Goal of Agricultural Policy?" "How
Do Farm People Live in Comparison with City People?"; "What Should Farmers Aim to Accomplish
through Organization?"

Taeusch points out that the local discussion groups are
not limited to the subjects prescribed by the department
and that most of them, in the course of a year, go in for
a good many unprescribed discussions: taxes, foreign
policy, the relationship between the farmer and the la-
borer, and others on which the government feels hesitant about supplying the material.

"What we are interested in," he said, "is to bring
the farmers abreast of the times and help them to see
that they can go a long way if they make up their minds
and go together."

If, up to the present, there has been no dramatic evidence of united action on this elaborately organized farm
front it is because the demands of the farmers, unlike
those of organized labor, have found substantial ful-
fillment. The agricultural policy of the administration,
unlike its labor policy, has taken money directly from
the Federal Treasury and put it in the pockets of the
working farmers of the nation. Organized labor, even
though it has had the benediction of the administration,
had had to go out and fight for what it wanted, whereas
agriculture, although now organized for fighting, has
had to do little of it.

But let those who make and preside over our national

agricultural policies become neglectful of or indifferent to these problems of farm prices and farm income, or seek to balance the budget by cutting off the farmers' benefits and we would have action on the united farm front as dramatic and as effective as that which has developed on the labor front. The threat of such action has already been sufficient to frighten Congress out of its recently publicized economy resolutions. When, early in May 1937, the Department of Agriculture's $925,000,000 appropriation bill came up in the House, a Republican representative moved to lop off 10 percent of it. Organized agriculture won the ensuing skirmish without having to fire a shot. Only thirty-two members of the House voted for the reduction.

It is evidence of that kind which accounts for the assurance in the Department of Agriculture that four years of missionary and organizational work among the farmers have borne significant fruit. The farmers are getting together and making up their minds. It is too soon to say what the results will be. Julian Friant, Mr. Wallace's astute dispenser of patronage, who has watched these developments with a more than friendly eye, believes that they will be apparent in 1940—the next Presidential year. He would not claim that this first period has made Democrats of the Republican farmers of the North. But I think he would agree that it has shown the farmers, north and south, some of the economic advantages to be gained by shopping around and that it has instructed them in both the point of view and the technique of ticket-splitting. They have learned what they want and have been provided with the machinery through which to ask for it. Their interest in political parties is on the wane. Their determination to get more of what they have had in the last four years is waxing.

The evangelists in the Department of Agriculture, even with three and a half more years at their disposal, may not be able to put Henry Wallace in the White House. But they can be depended upon to get the farmers of the nation in a position to see to it that the man who is put there and the platform on which he arrives both bear the stamp of their approval.

Meanwhile, there is no doubt at all of the fact that the New Deal farm program has built one of the most formidable class organizations in the history of American government and that to-day—Henry Wallace, mild, unobtrusive and as otherworldly as any man who ever held a Cabinet post, sits at the head and on top of it.

CHAPTER VIII

THE ROOSEVELT LABOR MOVEMENT

As LABOR statesmen, John L. Lewis and Franklin D. Roosevelt see eye to eye on almost everything of importance. As individuals they do not get along.

The fact that they do not get along is not because either man is hard to get along with. Socially, Mr. Lewis is considerably less hearty than Mr. Roosevelt. It takes him a longer time to get to a first-name basis with his acquaintances. He is sometimes exceedingly glum and sometimes exceedingly grim. But, given a good day, he makes a visitor feel as much at home in his red-plush, oak-paneled office in the Tower Building in Washington as the President in his whitewashed, circular office at the White House.

One of Mr. Lewis' associates told me the story of a young man who, one night in Washington, found himself at a dinner party with the chief of the CIO. Mr. Lewis was more than affable. He was the life of the affair. Encouraged by such apparently spontaneous unbending, the young man introduced himself to Mr. Lewis and said:

"If you don't mind my saying so I'm amazed. How is it that you're so gay to-night and yet that you're always so fierce in your pictures?"

Mr. Lewis put a finger to his mouth.

"Shhh," he said, "it's my business to look that way in my pictures."

The incompatibility between Mr. Lewis and Mr. Roosevelt is due, therefore, to no lack of the social graces. It is due, rather, to the fact that the country is not big enough for two men of destiny, going the same way, at the same time. If John L. Lewis had lived at the same time as Samuel Gompers or John Mitchell, I am sure that Mr. Roosevelt would look at him, in retrospect, as the greatest of labor leaders. And if Franklin D. Roosevelt were merely a prophet-in-prospect, I am sure that Mr. Lewis would find it easy to give him a top place among the coming great. It is the fact that the two men are contemporaries that makes it difficult.

Both men are individualists—classic illustrations of the tradition of rugged individualism that they both discount. They both give orders more acceptably than they take them. Both men are nonconformists in thought and insurgents in action. Mr. Lewis' self-confidence may be a shade less mystical than Mr. Roosevelt's but the results, for those who disagree, are about the same in both cases. No stargazer has described what happens to the planetary bodies which are presumed to follow and fix the destinies of men when two such cosmic personalities get together within the confines of a single earthly office. But it is fairly well known that their meetings, judged by mundane standards, are not love feasts— even though food is served. Both men are aware that they are going the same way and that they are more likely to get there if they go together. But the fact that they cannot get along without each other makes it that much more difficult for them to get along with each other.

When it comes to a labor gospel, however, they both use the same version. Both men believe that America's working people get too small a share of the income of American industry. They both believe that a fair share— along with decent working conditions—will never come about through the voluntary benevolence of the nation's employers; that it will have to be brought about—generally by strikes or the threat of strikes—through the organized strength of the nation's workers. Mr. Roosevelt has been obliged, for political reasons, to maintain his friendship with the American Federation of Labor. But I do not believe that he has any more sympathy with the conservative, Gompers-Green tradition of the A. F. of L. than Mr. Lewis. Both men want to see labor in politics and I think that both of them—if neither of the present parties proves to be a worthy custodian of labor's hopes—would look forward with some pleasure to the formation of a bona-fide labor party.

If, economically, Lewis seems farther to the left than Mr. Roosevelt it is because he wants to move fast and he has only the labor front to think about. Mr. Roosevelt also wants to move fast. But he has more than labor to think about.

It is probable that Mr. Roosevelt, if he were head of the CIO, would run it exactly as Mr. Lewis is running it, and that he would ignore his critics with the same eloquence or answer them, when the occasion called for it, with the same scorn. Mr. Roosevelt is no more against extremism than Mr. Lewis and he is just as aware that in such a movement, going at such a pace, some extremism is unavoidable. Mr. Roosevelt—despite the importuning of some of the Democratic Conservatives on Capitol Hill—did not speak out on the sit-down strikes. He did not speak out because if he had spoken his speech would have been a Lewis speech and not the kind his excited Democrats were clamoring for.

There is very little prospect of a permanent political break between the two. The reasons are obvious. Mr. Lewis' program needs Mr. Roosevelt's kind of an administration. And Mr. Roosevelt's program needs Mr. Lewis' kind of support. Those reasons were potent enough to cement their alliance in 1936. They are likely to continue to be potent enough to keep the alliance intact up to and, perhaps, even through the New Deal's test vote in 1940.

The labor record of the First New Deal is impressive. Never before had organized labor had an administration so openly friendly. And never, in any previous four years' period, had so many measures, favorable to labor, been enacted into law. The first of the successive legislative aids to labor was contained in the famous Section 7a of the National Industrial Recovery Act. This section was not revolutionary—despite the uproar that it aroused. It merely sought to bring industrial relations in the United States abreast of most of the rest of the civilized world by giving to labor the right to organize and bargain collectively through representatives of its own choosing.

In August 1933, the administration appointed the National Labor Board—the first national agency authorized to handle labor disputes. Having no statutory standing and no enforcement power, the Board's only weapon was persuasion. In August 1934, the National Labor Board was superseded by the National Labor Relations Board which was given a quasi-judicial standing. At the same time special boards were created for mediation purposes in the steel and textile industries and for the longshoremen's unions. At about the same time the Railway Labor Act was amended by Congress in such a way as to strengthen the collective bargaining rights of railway labor.

Doubtless the most important contribution of the National Labor Relations Board to labor progress in this period was its continued insistence upon the right of collective bargaining—an insistence which prepared the way for legislation under the Wagner Labor Relations Act. In the historic Houde Engineering Case, the Board held—for the first time—that an employer must accept the organization of a majority of his employees as the sole bargaining agency for all his employees.

In May 1935, the N.R.A. was declared unconstitutional. In June 1935, however, the labor gains of the N.R.A. were largely protected by the enactment of the Labor Relations Act. This Act created a National Labor Relations Board of three members. It guaranteed the right of collective bargaining. It specifically prevented the interference, by an employer, in the efforts of his employees to organize. This law—like all preceding liberal labor legislation, was bitterly fought by many employers of labor. But its validation by the Supreme Court, early in 1937, cleared it of any Constitutional doubts and left employers no alternative but to accept it as the new basis for capital-labor relations for all firms whose business is interstate.

But of more importance to labor than the New Deal's laws was the New Deal atmosphere. The Washington dice which, from time immemorial, had been loaded for the industrialists were reloaded—this time for labor.

It is true that old-time labor leaders did not think so

when Mr. Roosevelt, overriding all their objections and turning down all their nominations, appointed Miss Frances Perkins as Secretary of Labor. Miss Perkins was something new in the way of Secretaries of Labor, not because she was a woman but because she was not one of the superannuates of organized labor with whom the A. F. of L. had previously filled the post. It is not particularly high praise of Miss Perkins to say that she is probably a better Labor Secretary than any of her predecessors. She has had, from the very beginning of her tenure of office, a bad press—due to her mishandling of the newspaper men rather than to her mishandling of the problems of labor. Despite her long experience in public life the sight of a reporter still frightens her. Moreover—and unlike a good many other New Deal administrators—she is not gregarious or affable. She is absent-minded, finds it difficult to remember names or— for that matter—appointments. Her consistently late arrival at all the affairs which she is expected to attend —including even Cabinet meetings—has become something of a New Deal tradition.

Miss Perkins did not exactly cover herself with glory in the epidemic of strikes in the spring of 1937. Neither, for that matter, did the President of the United States or Ed. McGrady, the Assistant Secretary of Labor, who learned labor politics as a lobbyist for the A. F. of L. and is probably the best trouble shooter that the government has ever had at its disposal. The political situation be-

tween Mr. Lewis and Mr. Roosevelt being what it was
in the spring of 1937, it is exceedingly unlikely that any
Washington official could have acted differently or done
much more than Miss Perkins.

The Labor Department, however, is something more
than a mediation agency. It is a year-round activity of
the government with a vast number of administrative
responsibilities. No one who has had any current contact with the Department and who remembers its down-
at-the-heels status in previous administrations will question that Miss Perkins has brought it out of the bog and
made it a smooth-running, effective piece of governmental machinery. Her Brain Trust—headed by Isidor
Lubin, statistician—is as good as any in Washington.
And unlike some of the others it does not have to give
any of its thought to the sponsorship of a Presidential
boom for "the chief."

Miss Perkins, if she desires it, is almost sure to be the
Secretary of Labor as long as Mr. Roosevelt is President. This is partly due to the fact that the President
dislikes to make major changes in personnel and almost
never makes such changes when the people concerned
are under fire. It is due, also, to the fact that Miss Perkins has lost none of the intimacy of her relationship
with Mrs. Roosevelt. But, more important than these
reasons, Mr. Roosevelt is likely to keep Miss Perkins
because he knows that—even though she does not smoke
black cigars, slap the backs of all comers, and keep open

house at her office for labor's lobbyists—she has done a first-rate job in running the business of her department.

Miss Perkins is very much a part of the friendly atmosphere with which labor has been surrounded by the New Deal. She has never paid dues to a union. But her sympathies are none-the-less pro-union, probably more intelligently so than if she had had all her labor experience inside the ranks of industry.

But if organized labor had grounds to complain because Miss Perkins was not "one of the boys" it had very little else to complain about. "The boys" began to have their innings—as they had never hoped for—soon after Mr. Roosevelt took office. Friends of labor and labor leaders began to move in from all directions. Harry Hopkins was Federal Relief Administrator. Bob Wagner was the Presidential spokesman on labor questions in the Senate, John L. Lewis was on the Labor Board of the N.R.A. So was Sidney Hillman, President of the Amalgamated Clothing Workers of America and for a long time the brains of the more aggressive labor movement. So also were Leo Wolman, pro-labor Professor at Columbia University, and Donald R. Richberg, Chicago labor lawyer. Rexford Guy Tugwell and Adolph Berle were pro-labor Brain Trusters. Felix Frankfurter was an absentee consultant. Jerome Frank, another liberal Chicago lawyer, was in at the Department of Agriculture; Jimmy Landis, a Frankfurter product, soon appeared at the Securities Exchange Commission; David

Lilienthal, another Frankfurter discovery, came in with the Tennessee Valley Authority. And, Mrs. Roosevelt—although never formally identified with the organized labor movement—was actively interested in such organizations as the Woman's Trade Union League and numbered such effective women labor leaders as Rose Schneideman and Eleanor Herrick among her close friends. And, somewhat lower in the scale, there were embattled battalions of young men and women whose knowledge of the problems of labor was limited but whose highly articulate pro-labor opinions helped to make it evident that Mr. Roosevelt's election had been a labor triumph.

It was in this atmosphere and during the life of the N.R.A. that some of the more imaginative labor leaders —notably John L. Lewis and Sidney Hillman—began to think long thoughts about the movement. The A. F. of L. had badly bungled its chance under the N.R.A. It hailed section 7a as the Magna Charta for labor and then did nothing about it. As a result shrewd employers got busy and began to put company unions in the field which the Federation should have occupied. Lewis and Hillman watched this protracted bungling with increasing disgust. They knew that Mr. Roosevelt had little sympathy for company unions; that his hope, with the 7a, was a forward-surging national labor movement. They knew, moreover, that Mr. Roosevelt's liberal program depended in large part for its success upon such a movement. The President did not deliberately sponsor the organization of Lewis' Committee for Industrial Organization. But—lacking a rebirth of the A. F. of L. —his policies made it inevitable.

The labor issue in the 1936 campaign involved much more than the fate of Mr. Roosevelt's further reforms. It involved the fate of the Roosevelt-Lewis philosophy of the labor movement. The American Federation of Labor supported Mr. Roosevelt because of what he had done in the field of labor legislation. That, also, had something to do with Mr. Lewis' support. But Mr. Lewis did more than support the President. He fought for him and backed his fighting with half a million dollars from the treasury of the United Mine Workers of America. It was not primarily because of the New Deal's legislation that he did that. He did it because he believed that, with four more years of Mr. Roosevelt in the White House substance would be given to his dream of a national vertically organized labor movement, powerful enough to defy both the A. F. of L. and the management of the nation's unorganized industries and politically articulate enough to be a decisive election factor in certain states and almost that in the nation.

John L. Lewis, without doubt, was the largest single question in the minds of the Democratic strategists in the last campaign. William Green, President of the A. F. of L., was somewhat ineffectively for the President. Some of his associate executives, notably George Harrison of the Railway Unions, were more aggressive. The Democratic National Committee set up a labor division under the direction of an old A. F. of L. official. But the Roosevelt hope for a bloc delivery of the labor vote centered almost entirely in John L. Lewis. And there were times when it looked as though that hope might be ill-founded.

For one thing, and despite all he had at stake, it was no simple matter to keep Lewis on the reservation. When, in the late spring of 1936, the Lewis-sponsored Guffey Coal Bill was defeated after what appeared to be only half-hearted White House efforts to save it, he all but packed his bags for a trip into political seclusion from which, until after election, he swore he would not return. But a meeting was arranged with Mr. Roosevelt and however towering Lewis' rage may have been when the meeting began, it had entirely vanished by its conclusion, under the warm smile and, more to the point, the definite assurances of the President. I do not think that Mr. Lewis took any written agreement away from that meeting. But I am sure that he heard, there, a rather full outline of the Second New Deal. At any rate, what he heard appeared, amply, to satisfy him and from that time on he was regular as Jim Farley.

Another major scare appeared on the labor front when, in the closing days of the campaign, the Republicans unleashed their pay-envelope propaganda in which employers of labor warned their employees that if Mr.

ROOSEVELT—*And Then?*

Roosevelt were reëlected his Social Security Act would cost them a regular deduction from their pay. Most of the Republicans' high explosives, up to that point, had been duds. This one, however, precipitated a near-panic in the Democratic high command. Reports came in from industrial cities of streets near the gates of factories which were covered with Roosevelt buttons discarded by disillusioned workmen; of Roosevelt stickers torn from cars and Roosevelt posters removed from the windows of stores in industrial districts. It looked bad—so bad that for a week practically every wheel in the Democratic campaign machine was turning out material to meet it and the President, himself, discussed the question in every one of the last four or five speeches of his campaign.

I do not believe that Mr. Lewis was very much disturbed. He was looking after Pennsylvania at the time and I think he realized that the job of selling Mr. Roosevelt's administration had been done too well to be undone by any such last minute attacks. As it turned out, of course, he was right. What he had promised labor would do labor overwhelmingly did. Labor went down the line with Mr. Lewis for Mr. Roosevelt. It is too soon to say which of the two gained most from the victory. Mr. Roosevelt got a second term in the White House. But Mr. Lewis got a labor movement which, being the nearest thing to a labor party that American politics has seen in many decades, may quite possibly be putting men in the White House or keeping them out of it long after Mr. Roosevelt has departed.

Mr. Lewis, of course, had had his taste of political triumph before 1936. The state of Pennsylvania, since it is the seat of strength of the United Mine Workers of America, has always been his favorite bailiwick. His following was a force to be reckoned with in that state long before the advent of Mr. Roosevelt and the Guffey-Earle combination that followed in the Roosevelt train. But until Mr. Roosevelt and 1932 the state remained safely Republican. In 1932 it remained Republican but it ceased to be safe. In 1934 George Earle, a political and economic renegade from the Philadelphia Social Registry, carried the New Deal into the Gubernatorial Mansion, Joe Guffey, the tight-lipped, hoarse-voiced boss of the Democratic State machine, carried it into the United States Senate, and Dave Lawrence, Guffey's smooth chairman of the Democratic State Committee carried it into all the available public offices, and into a good many unavailable ones. After nearly three generations of leanness, the sleek and fattened Democracy of Pennsylvania carried the state for the President in 1936.

It was the fact that the Pennsylvania Democrats simultaneously had a John L. Lewis and a Franklin D. Roosevelt that made that historic triumph. It is quite probable that Pennsylvania would go Democratic in 1940, without Mr. Roosevelt. It is not possible for it to go Democratic in 1940 without Mr. Lewis. The voice that speaks for Pennsylvania may be the voice of Guffey or Earle. But the hand which holds the ballots which will swing that state's thirty-six electoral votes is the hand of John L. Lewis.

But just as Mr. Lewis is no longer limited, in his labor activities, to the United Mine Workers, so he is no longer limited, in his political efforts, to the state of Pennsylvania. He was by no means limited to it in the last campaign. He was—and still is—the guiding genius and energizing force behind Labor's Non-Partisan League. And Labor's Non-Partisan League, if it does not enter the field with a third party ticket in 1940, is sure to be in a position to put the Democrats and the Republicans on an embarrassing spot in that year and cause widespread headaches among all the important candidates. In the last election it was probably the most effective pro-Roosevelt political machine outside of the Democratic National Committee. One indication of how effectively it served is found in the appointment of its out-in-front man, Major George L. Berry to the United States Senate to fill the vacancy left by the death of Tennessee's Senator N. L. Bachman. Major Berry, since 1907, has been President of the International Pressmen and Assistants Union of North America. As Mr. Roosevelt's pre-campaign "Coördinator for Industrial Coöperation," he was alternately an asset and a liability to the President. But he was irrepressible and

determined and, when the campaign finally got under
way, he contributed, significantly, to what proved to be
the most complete mobilization of the labor vote in
American political history.

Major Berry, since he has taken his seat in the Senate,
has resigned as President of Labor's Non-Partisan
League. But the League, still blessed by Mr. Lewis
and presumably, also, by Mr. Roosevelt, continues to
carry on. In fact, since the election the significance of
its activities has considerably increased. It is not a third
party. Not yet. It is rather, the political machinery
through which organized labor, both A. F. of L. and
CIO labor, can bring its united political influence to
bear in local, state, and national elections and upon state
legislatures and Congress.

The machinery, itself, is an indication of how far
labor has come politically since the Samuel Gompers
period. Every state in the union is organized, with a
functioning state committee. The 48 state committees
include nearly fifteen hundred people in their membership. In every industrial state the machinery has been
brought down through district committees to organization in the counties and cities. In a number of more important industrial cities, there are precinct organizations
set up on a block basis, with precinct and block captains.
This is the case, for example, in the city of New York
where there are 100 Assembly District organizations,
with precinct and block captains for every one of them.

Denver and Pittsburgh are similarly organized. Of all the states, Pennsylvania is the most completely organized. By the spring of 1936—eight months after the League launched its permanent organizing campaign—it had enrolled more than 34,000 active precinct, county, and state workers throughout the nation.

Seventy-five percent of these active workers are affiliated with some labor union—either CIO or A. F. of L. Of the 48 state chairmen, 21 are members of CIO unions and 27 members of A. F. of L. unions. Of the 48 state secretaries, 36 are A. F. of L. men and 12 are CIO. More than fifty A. F. of L. and CIO unions have officially affiliated with the League and have representatives on the National Executive Board. The membership of these represented unions totals something more than two and a half million.

The organization is financed by individual contributions and by assessments made by various unions upon their members. By April 1936, the records of the League showed that not fewer than a million people were contributing—either personally or through the vote of their unions—to the League's treasury.

The League—like the British Labor Party—has a rather considerable support among the liberal intellectuals. It has established a working relationship with the North Carolina League for Progressive Legislation which, with its headquarters at Chapel Hill, has a number of college professors in its leadership. Other somewhat similar groups, made up in large part of professional people, are unofficially coöperating with the League in Pennsylvania, Ohio, Wisconsin, and Iowa.

The men behind the League never had any doubt of their ability to get the support of labor. It is their aim, however, to go beyond that and enlist an important bloc of the nation's farmers. They have had some success. At the League's first national convention, which brought 200 accredited delegates to Washington in March 1936, the Farmers' Union—an aggressively pro-New Deal organization chiefly among wheat farmers—had official representatives on hand from four states. In the national drive which the League sponsored in behalf of Mr. Roosevelt's Supreme Court proposal, farm and labor spokesmen united in many of the mass meetings. And at the League's offices in the Willard Hotel in Washington there have been innumerable, unreported conferences between the official representatives of organized labor and the official representatives of organized agriculture. In fact, the Secretary of the League told me that, within six months after the election, officers from practically every important farm organization in the country had visited the League's headquarters and discussed with its officials the problems of a closer political alliance between labor and agriculture.

In anticipation of the 1938 elections—and the test cases which the League will attempt to pull off in that year—there has been formed a Farmers' Non-Partisan

League. The individual behind this organization is William M. Thatcher. Thatcher has been the moving spirit in the Farmers' Union. He is close to Mr. Wallace and can be counted on to make an agricultural showing for Mr. Wallace's policies when all other farm leaders fail.

The Farmers' Non-Partisan League is, in effect, the agricultural wing of Labor's Non-Partisan League. Just as the L.N.P.L. has gone into New York City—where its chance to make a showing is better than in most places—so the F.N.P.L. plans to concentrate on such states as Minnesota, the Dakotas, Iowa, Nebraska, and Montana.

No one, of course, believes that outside of such states there is likely to be any very close alliance between labor and agriculture as early as the 1938 elections. In general, class-conscious agriculture does not yet recognize that it has a community of economic and therefore of political interest with class-conscious labor. But such recognition, I think, is on the way. And it is the aim of Labor's Non-Partisan League and of this recently formed affiliate to speed its coming.

This large and steadily expanding machinery for the concentrating of the political power of American labor is a definite and formidable expression of the political and economic philosophy of Mr. Roosevelt and Mr. Lewis. Mr. Roosevelt, quite as much as Mr. Lewis, desires to accomplish certain things for American labor and he is quite as much aware as Mr. Lewis of the fact that those things cannot be accomplished or their accomplishment safeguarded without a highly organized, highly political labor movement. As I have already pointed out, the specific policies of the New Deal and, even more, the New Deal atmosphere were designed, in part at least, to bring such a movement into being. The CIO is the industrial fruit of that purpose and Labor's Non-Partisan League is its political fruit.

Mr. Roosevelt is undoubtedly a better Democrat than Mr. Lewis—who is no Democrat at all. But Mr. Lewis' distrust of the old-order Democratic party as a fit vehicle for labor progress is probably no greater than Mr. Roosevelt's. In the end, if Mr. Roosevelt has his way, the old-order Democracy will cease to be and we will have a new party which—even though it bears the old name—will be a party in which both aggressive labor and aggressive agriculture can unhesitatingly put their trust. Meanwhile, the existence outside of the party of a political machine like this is bound to have great influence on those Democrats whose New Deal liberalism is maintained only under political duress.

I feel certain that Mr. Roosevelt—despite his Supreme Court defeat—is confident that, by 1940, he can make the Democratic Party enough of Mr. Lewis' kind of party to keep the CIO, Labor's Non-Partisan League and a considerable number of other organizations whose politics they influence on the New Deal reservation. This, of course, involves a 1940 platform and, more important, a 1940 candidate satisfactory to Mr. Lewis.

If Mr. Roosevelt carries out his purpose to pick the candidate he will probably seek to find a man made more in the likeness of Lewis than of any of the traditional Democrats. He will do that simply because he will probably have made up his mind that, for its long-time importance, the Roosevelt program stands in greater need of the kind of support that Mr. Lewis can rally than of the apparently more significant backing of the party's conservatives. He is well aware of the fact that a good many of the party's conservatives would support the ticket for the party's sake whereas Mr. Lewis would only support it because he was satisfied with what it offered.

The question has been frequently raised as to whether Mr. Lewis, in 1940, could be satisfied with a ticket which was not headed by Mr. Lewis. I do not take Mr. Lewis' ambitions lightly. But I do not believe that they include the Presidency—not, at any rate, in that year. He is too shrewd an operator to take any such unnecessary and premature risks. He is one of the relatively few men of importance in Washington who is ready to classify himself with those whom the people of the United States in 1940 will not make President. He believes that the American people will elect a man who is friendly to labor. He proposes to have a good deal to do in picking the man and in electing him. But I do not think that he believes the American people are ready, yet, to elect a labor man.

It is altogether possible, of course, that the Democratic party, in the next Presidential year, will not be satisfactory to labor. It is almost certain that the Republican party will not be. In that event labor, with what other liberal forces it could rally, would undoubtedly put its own ticket in the field. The question of a new party is—as all the politically minded labor leaders frankly declare—an open question. Politics has begun to get into labor's blood and there is a strong and, I should say, increasing group in the labor movement— in the A. F. of L. as well as the CIO—which wants a new party regardless of what the other parties do. But that group is not likely to have its way unless Mr. Roosevelt's labor legislation is permanently blocked, his political fortunes given a set-back in 1938, and an anti-New Deal faction captures control of the Democratic machinery in the 1940 convention.

In that case there would be a third party with a vengeance. Such a party probably would not expect to carry the election. But it would take away that vast number of voters who have made the Democratic Party the majority party in a number of heretofore Republican states such as Pennsylvania and California and that would probably be defection enough to bring in the Republicans. It is even conceivable, that such a third party, created from the scattered tribes of the New Deal, might win. To win—however—it would have to have Franklin D. Roosevelt for its candidate.

CHAPTER IX

THE NEGRO VOTE *versus* THE SOLID SOUTH

THE most remarkable gathering in the Presidential campaign of 1936 was a Negro mass meeting staged, in mid-October, in Madison Square Garden in New York City. The expenses of the meeting were largely met by the Democratic National Committee. But it was officially sponsored by the National Colored Committee of the Good Neighbor League.

The doors at the Garden, that night, were opened at seven o'clock. A handful of people drifted in and filled the first two rows of seats on the main floor. At seventhirty, it looked as though the dire predictions of the political wise men who had declared that New York City's Negroes would never come all the way from Harlem to attend a Democratic political rally would be fulfilled. By eight, however, Harlem began to appear. At nine o'clock the police were obliged to close the doors. The vast auditorium was packed, from the main floor to the fourth balcony, with 16,000 Negroes. What was subsequently described as the largest Negro political rally in the history of the country was under way.

It should be pointed out that the bait for that meeting was not entirely political. The Elks Band—Harlem's finest and most resplendent—was on hand. So was the much more expensive Cab Calloway and his orchestra. The radio-famous Elder Mischaux had brought his "I'm So Happy" choir all the way from Washington, robed them in lily-white gowns and seated them, in the form of a cross, on the platform. The Negro composer of "The St. Louis Blues" was there and played the song that made him famous. The platform fairly sagged with Negro bishops and church dignitaries.

Between the "Star Spangled Banner" and the Invocation—with which the meeting opened—and "America" and the Benediction with which, at nearly midnight, it concluded, there was plenty of politics. But it was pleasantly seasoned politics. Senator Robert F. Wagner and Representative Caroline O'Day and Donald R. Richberg all had their say. Bishop Reverdy C. Ransome, of the African Methodist Episcopal Church, read a New Emancipation Proclamation (the meeting was held, incidentally, on a date widely celebrated in certain Negro communities as Emancipation Day). But these strictly political appeals were all properly separated from each other by exhibitions of Cab Calloway's "truckin'," demonstrations of Elder Mischaux' altar-call technique and a variety of other divertissements. The 16,000 stayed to the end and returned to Harlem after one of the best free shows on record. Most of them—and most of their 350,000 Negro neighbors in Harlem—subsequently voted for Mr. Roosevelt.

But the most important part of that night's demonstration of Negro solidarity was not made in New York City, but in sixty other cities of the country in which similar mass meetings were simultaneously held. A half hour of the high-spot part of the Madison Square Garden meeting was broadcast over a coast-to-coast radio network—with all southern stations carefully omitted from the hook-up. No estimate was ever made of the total number of Negroes who had assembled in these sixty other Roosevelt Emancipation Day gatherings. But it is safe to say that the Negroes of the North had never before joined in so great a show of political strength. The banner headlines and full page stories in the Negro press were indicative of the impression that was made. And a more significant indication appeared, a few weeks later, when most of the nation's northern Negroes deserted their traditional allegiance to the Republican party and voted Democratic.

It was fairly evident, long before these meetings, that the Negroes of the North would vote for Mr. Roosevelt. They—and many of their racial brethren in the South—were high up among the New Deal's beneficiaries. Mr. Roosevelt had gone farther than most of his predecessors in giving recognition to outstanding Negroes. An honest and generally successful effort had been made to eliminate racial discrimination in the various emergency projects. The Roosevelts, and particularly Mrs. Roosevelt, numbered a considerable number of the benefactors of the Negro race among their friends. The Roosevelt philosophy looked like the "Second Emancipation," to which Bishop Ransome referred at the Madison Square Garden meeting. Months before the campaign was under way the President was already being hailed as the new Abraham Lincoln. In fact, the biggest cheer of the evening, at Madison Square Garden, came at the moment when Elder Mischaux dramatically unveiled a vast portrait of the President—with a company of Negroes bowing before him and the spirit of Lincoln hovering in the background.

The First New Deal—up to June 1, 1936—had employed 25,000 Negro young men and women in its National Youth Administration projects. For the years 1936-1937, it had appropriated $75,000 for the use of colored graduate students. In 1935, its appropriations for the aid of Negro young people in college amounted to $600,000. More than a million dollars was appropriated for Negro students in lower schools; 21,000 high school students were doing part-time work for the NYA. And the NYA, itself, had 28 Negro assistant state directors and 28 colored people on state advisory committees. The Director of Negro work, under the NYA, was

Mrs. Mary McLeod Bethune, President of Bethune-Cookman College, Daytona Beach, Florida, and perhaps, the most widely influential Negro woman in America.

Similarly, more than 200,000 Negro young men have gone through the camps of the Civilian Conservation Corps and nearly 150 Negro college graduates are serving in these camps as educational advisers. Under the Public Works Administration, the New Deal granted $3,000,000 to Howard University; $7,500,000 for Negro schools and colleges in fifteen southern states; and undertook nineteen housing projects for colored residents. Up to the first of June 1936, more than 1,000,000 colored people had enrolled in the government's emergency education classes, and 300,000 of them had been taught to read and write. President Roosevelt had approved the appropriation of $650,000 for a Negro-conducted study of Negro education in the United States and $470,000 for a survey of the Occupational Status of Negroes. In June 1936, 300,000 colored people were engaged as unskilled workers in various WPA projects—in addition to 30,000 women and 20,000 skilled workers.

It was not difficult—with such a record—to mobilize the Negro vote, persuade it to cut loose from its traditional Republicanism and go down the line at the election for Mr. Roosevelt. But the President had more in his favor than the record. His point of view, his language, the objectives to which he dedicated himself were almost identical with the gospel that for two generations had been preached in a thousand Negro pulpits by the religious leaders of the race. The President talked about under-privilege, about injustice, about long working hours and poor pay and bad housing; about child labor and under-nourishment and inadequate clothes. The Negroes of the United States knew about all of those things. They were suffering from them. Their preachers had cried out—unavailingly—against them. And here, at last, was a President who not only was aroused—as the preachers were aroused—but who was actually doing something about it. Small wonder that they were stirred. This was the dawning of the day for which they had waited.

Politically, however, the Negro swing to Mr. Roosevelt and—temporarily at least to the Democrats—was significant because it indicated, first, that there is such a thing in the North, as Negro political solidarity and, second, that the Negro vote is not necessarily determined any longer by either habit or tradition. For the time being the Democrats believe that in a good many northern states they have swallowed up a large proportion of hitherto Republican Negroes. But they are not too sure of it. The northern Negro did not demonstrate, in the last election, that he was a Democrat. He demonstrated that he was a free lance. His leaders—and particularly his religious leaders—who generally have more political influence than the politicians—are at the point, now, where they propose to make up their own minds on political and economic questions. They are becoming aware of their electoral importance. If they seek to deliver the vote it will be because—in terms of benefits for their people—they have got a price for it.

They have a great belief in Mr. Roosevelt. They look upon him as a Deliverer. I think that they are likely to stay with the Democrats as long as the Democrats continue to talk his language and support his kind of legislation. But in the event that the conservative Democrats of the solid South once again gain control of the party, then the Negro vote—a large bloc of it, at least—can be counted upon to support the third party movement which would almost inevitably follow such a resurgence of conservatism. If Mr. Roosevelt, himself, should lead such a third-party movement or give it his blessing, then I think an overwhelming majority of the North's four million Negro voters would support it.

The organization of the Negro vote into an effective political bloc, which began under the stimulus of the First New Deal, has made considerable progress since the last election. Most of that progress has been accomplished under the auspices of the National Negro Congress.

The National Negro Congress has its national headquarters in three modest offices on the second floor of a second-rate building on Florida Avenue in Washington, D. C. The national President of the Congress is A. Phillip Randolph. Mr. Randolph is also the President of the International Brotherhood of Sleeping Car Porters and close to John L. Lewis. The Executive Secretary of the Congress—and the man who makes its wheels revolve—is a 32-year-old Negro by the name of John P. Davis. Davis is a graduate of Bates College and of the Harvard Law School. At Harvard he was a protégé of Felix Frankfurter and a friend of Jimmy Landis—an earlier Frankfurter man who was subsequently made chairman of the Securities and Exchange Commission. Davis, who was a Hoover Republican in 1928, came to Washington in the early days of the Roosevelt administration and got a job with the N.R.A. He moved into the present job in 1935.

The National Negro Congress is the outgrowth of a Negro Economic Conference which was held at Howard University in Washington in May 1935. At that time the spokesmen for a considerable number of Negro organizations, recognizing the need of some politically coördinating body, agreed to coöperate in the establishment of the Congress. At the present time, 38 Negro organizations are represented on its Board of Directors or have given its work official endorsement.

In February 1936, the Congress held its first national meeting in Chicago. More than 1000 accredited delegates came to Chicago from every section of the country. More than 10,000 Negroes were present at the first session. This conference made no party-political declarations. Mr. Randolph brought forward a resolution of endorsement for the Farmer-Labor party—a resolution which would almost certainly have passed—but was persuaded to withdraw it in order to maintain, for the time being, the nonpartisan character of the organization.

The present nonpartisan position of the Congress is largely a result of Mr. Davis' influence. Davis, of course, has been hailed as a radical. That, however, is largely a result of the fact that he has brains and is realistic. He believes—as he outlined his point of view to me—that all the Negroes of the nation, north and south, have a community of economic and political interest. He does not believe that they can depend for their progress upon the occasional waves of good-will and liberalism that may sweep through the nation. He quotes John L. Lewis and insists that the Negroes in the long-run, will never get any more political and economic advantages than they are in a position to demand. It is his aim, through the National Congress, to get them in a state of organization so effective that what they demand they will be likely to get. That is why he does not believe that the Congress should tie up permanently to any party but, rather, that it should keep itself in a position to go into action on any front and on any issue where the interests of the nation's Negroes are involved.

At the time I talked with Mr. Davis he had just swung the machinery of the Congress into action in support of the President's Supreme Court plan. In this activity—significantly enough—Davis was working in close coöperation with Labor's Non-Partisan League. The pamphlet which the Congress was distributing on the subject declared, on its title page: "Shall the Supreme Court Continue to Ignore the 14th and 15th Amendments? Join the Fight to Guarantee to the Negro People their Rights under the Constitution by supporting the Supreme Court Modernization Plan." Underneath these captions there was a photograph of Abraham Lincoln.

In the Negro case against the Court, advanced by this pamphlet, it was pointed out that "this same Court upheld the right of states to pass Jim-Crow car laws. . . . The Supreme Court by its decisions has enforced schemes to create Jim-Crow residential areas for Negroes. . . . Every major citizenship right guaranteed to Negroes by the 14th Amendment has been crippled by the Court so that in reality Negro people are able to enjoy only a small portion of their legal rights. . . . More than three million qualified Negro voters are denied any effective means of using their vote by the Supreme Court interpretation of the 15th Amendment. . . . The Negro people, joining hands with the forces of progress, with the mighty forces of labor in this country, must see to it that the will of the people is accomplished. . . . Write to your Senators and Congressmen."

Davis, however, believes that the most important immediate steps toward Negro solidarity must be taken in the field of industrial organization. He is considerably closer to the CIO than to the A. F. of L. simply because he is against racial discrimination in labor organizations and he believes that the policy of the CIO on this point is more liberal than that of the A. F. of L. But Davis, as I have said, is a realist. He does not believe that the Negro workers should join the unions only after all discriminations against them have been removed.

"If we kept out of the unions for that reason then we ought, with equal reason, to keep out of the churches. Our program is to start where we are and to work toward what we want—only we prefer to do our working from the inside."

Davis recognizes that the big problem ahead of his organization is the Negro of the South. On the basis of proportional representation, 70 percent of the delegates at the Chicago convention should have come from the South. As it was, only 15 percent were southern Negroes. The Congress, therefore, looks upon the South as a special problem and is making a special approach to it through the organization of a "Southern Negro Youth Congress," with headquarters in Richmond, Virginia. In February 1937, this Congress had its first all-southern convention of Negro young people. Practically every important Negro organization, including the Y.M.C.A., the Y.W.C.A., the various churches, the National Association for the Advancement of the Colored People, as well as spokesmen for organized labor, were represented at this meeting.

"The key to the organization of the South," says Davis, "is the younger generation of Negroes. They are on the way."

It is not likely that many of the southern conservatives in Congress are aware of the National Negro Congress. But the National Negro Congress is aware of them. If they were to drop in at the offices of the organization they could get detailed statistics to show just what the Negro workers of the South will do— when they are organized—to the white political dynasties that have been built there. In North Carolina, according to Davis, 20,000 Negroes voted in the 1936 election. "There will be more than 50,000 in 1940." In Texas, by 1940, it is the aim to mobilize 150,000 voters out of the state's 800,000 Negroes. "In Oklahoma, Kentucky and Tennessee we hope to hold the balance of power." If the CIO succeeds in organizing steel, "then Alabama will no longer be a certain part of the solid south." Only Georgia, South Carolina, and Mississippi are held to be safely solid.

But whether or not they are aware of the National

Negro Congress, a good many southern Senators and Representatives are acutely aware of what the First and Second New Deals are doing for and to the Negroes. In fact, they are so acutely aware of it—and of the consequent gulf that divides the New Deal from traditional Democracy—that the fight on the anti-lynching law in the 1937 session of Congress aroused more forebodings among southern Democrats than any of that session's legislative proposals including the Supreme Court plan. The anti-lynching law was supported in the Senate by New York's Robert F. Wagner and in the House by Joseph A. Gavagan, Democratic Representative whose district includes most of Harlem. It was an effort to repay—in legislative coin—the debt of the Democrats of the North to the Negro voters who deserted the Republicans in the last election.

When the bill came up, William B. Bankhead, of Alabama, the Speaker of the House, expressed the almost unanimous opinion of his southern colleagues when he said: "what Fort Sumter started will be only a picnic compared to what you boys are going to start with that anti-lynching bill." The bill passed in the House. The Senate did not act on it. But there was an impression on Capitol Hill that the White House looked on the bill with favor and that served to increase the conviction that—in the long run and on almost all fundamental matters—the New Deal and the solid South are wholly incompatible.

I have never discovered any great alarm among New Dealers at that prospect. In fact, I have heard statistically-minded supporters of the present administration set forth the facts which, presumably, prove that the surrender, by the New Deal, of the solid South in exchange for the Negro vote would be a very good trade. It was pointed out that the Negroes, in any close election, represent the balance of power in Pennsylvania, New York, Ohio, Michigan, and Illinois. The electoral votes of those states is 157. That is 31 votes more than the total electoral vote of the eleven states of the solid South.

No one—least of all the leaders of the Negro people—believes that the political and economic solidarity of the Negroes, even in the North, has as yet begun to approach the solidarity of the solid South. But, on the other hand, no one whom I have met who is at all familiar with what is going on among the nation's Negroes denies that a very effective solidarity is in the making. It has already gone far enough to make it certain that, in future elections, the Negro vote will come in for an even more intensive cultivation than it had in the last election. The political fact has at last been established that there is a Negro vote and, more important, that that vote is no longer bound by traditions but, henceforth, will increasingly be inclined to "shop around" among the parties.

For speeding this development the Roosevelt philosophy and the policies of the New Deal are largely responsible. Mr. Roosevelt, save on one occasion when he dedicated a building at Howard University, has never spoken directly to the Negroes of the nation. But almost everything he has said has appeared to put him on their side. And his policies have probably been of a direct benefit to a larger percentage of our Negro population than to any other group of citizens.

The New Deal drive among the Negroes in the last campaign—particularly in such states as New York, Pennsylvania, Ohio, and Illinois—made them more than ever aware not only of their political importance, but of their stake in the Roosevelt program. So far as objectives are concerned there is no doubt that such New Dealers as Senator Guffey and Governor Earle of Pennsylvania, Senator Wagner of New York, Senator Minton of Indiana and Governor Murphy of Michigan have more objectives in common with their Negro supporters than with many of their southern Democratic colleagues. That, I think, could also be said of Mr. Roosevelt.

CHAPTER X

THE NEO-NEW DEALERS

WHEN the time comes, as it will, when Mr. Roosevelt will be obliged, politically, to fish or cut bait—to make it clear what he proposes to do with the Democratic party or whether he proposes to do without it—he will find a bloc of do or die Congressmen in both the House and the Senate ready to follow in his train. That is, they will follow him provided it is plain that he proposes to continue on the same road on which he has been going. These men are not, strictly speaking, "coat-tail" Congressmen. They would not deny that they came in with Mr. Roosevelt. But a very short session with any of them indicates that they are thinking for themselves. The fact that their thoughts run along Mr. Roosevelt's lines is merely a fortunate political circumstance. If Mr. Roosevelt's line changed most of them, in my opinion, would refuse to change with him.

The more aggressive and the better organized bloc of these Congressmen is in the House. There is, however, a growing company of the same sort in the Senate. The leaders of the Senate group are Sherman Minton of Indiana, Lewis Schwellenbach of Washington, and Claude Pepper of Florida. It is significant of the shift in the center of gravity of the Democratic party that only one of these three is from the so-called solid South and he from the untypically southern state of Florida.

All three are first-term Senators. Minton's hard-hitting ability on the floor of the Senate and his irrepressible thick-and-thin support of the President lifted him out of first-term obscurity to the post of assistant leader to Albin Barkley. That is not only an almost unprecedented honor but, with the leadership in Barkley's hands, it indicates how far the party organization has swung from its conventional dependence upon conservative Southerners.

Schwellenbach is forty-three years old, a war veteran and a lawyer. His most dramatic achievement in the Senate, to date, was his single-handed breaking of a Huey Long filibuster. He is a left-wing New Dealer whose presence on the floor of the Senate is a guarantee that Mr. Roosevelt's policies will always have an aggressive defender and whose presence in the Democratic party is a further indication of the width of the gulf that has developed—within that party—between the North and the South.

Pepper, who was elected in 1936 to fill out the unexpired term of Duncan Fletcher, is only thirty-seven.

He is, among other things, a Phi Beta Kappa. Few Senators have taken a more active hand in the business of the Senate in their first session than Pepper. There are indications that the eye of the White House has been fixed on him with more than ordinary approval.

These three men have allied with them a considerable Senatorial group—some of them newcomers, a few of them old-time liberals. Together they constitute a significant nucleus of men who—though Democrats—are, first of all, New Dealers; whose commitment to the party is secondary to their commitment to certain definite political and economic objectives which happen to be, also, the objectives of Mr. Roosevelt.

But, as I have said, the more important organization of Roosevelt Democrats is in the House of Representatives. The appearance on the American political scene of the individuals in this organization is, I believe, one of the most important signs of the times. They are a phenomenon that has caused more than a little sleeplessness among the old-line Democrats and more than a little satisfaction to Mr. Roosevelt as he looks to and plans for the future—both his own and that of his New Deals. The story of this bloc—of the men who are in it and of what they are driving at—may turn out to be the preface to an entirely new chapter in American political history.

Signs in the old House office building at the National Capitol in Washington indicate that the elevators run from the subway to the fourth floor. Until recently I took it for granted that there were only four floors. But I have found out that there is a fifth. In fact, I was taken to the fifth floor not long ago by one of the few Congressmen who have keys and know where the stairs are.

The fifth floor, like the other four, is filled with offices. But the corridors are low, poorly lighted and empty. There are no uniformed guards to direct you and no names on the office doors. Each office opens out on a balcony that runs entirely around the inner court of the building. The offices, themselves, are small, two-by-four affairs with very little furniture, no telephones, no typewriters and no visiting constituents.

"This," said my guide, "is our Congressional hideout. Up here we have only one rule: nobody speaks to anybody. We don't know who our neighbors are and our neighbors don't know us. The place is reserved for Congressmen who like to get off alone, now and then, for serious study and heavy thinking."

This particular Congressman is obviously a member of the "heavy thinking" contingent. In his fifth floor room—as the well-thumbed books on his table indicated—he reads Montesquieu and Montague and Hume and, on the lighter side, Bryce and Beard and Adams. But he is not boastful about it and he is altogether too good a politician to parade his knowledge on the floor of the House, where an erudite man may be suspect. On the floor he flavors his arguments with the most up-to-date colloquialisms. If he makes quotations he picks them from such standard sources as Thomas Jefferson or the Bible. No one, listening to him in a hot debate, would get any hint of the intellectual company he keeps in his hide-out office or how far he has gone in his thinking beyond the objectives of the legislation that he may be currently fighting for.

He is young, confident, and astute. In the present session of Congress he is by no means a lonesome figure. On the contrary he is one of a group of like-minded Congressional youngsters. Many of them have not yet got fifth floor offices, but their applications are in. Meanwhile, they go in for heavy thinking off the floor and political shrewdness on it and, having found themselves in accord on most matters, have pooled their influence to form a bloc that makes up in determination and knowledge what it lacks in numbers.

In the 1936 session of Congress there were some twenty of them. In the 1937 session they mustered more than forty and they are getting recruits—some of them from among the older Congressmen. Most of them came in with Roosevelt, but very few of them would be willing to stop with him. They all support the New Deal, but they are thinking beyond it. Their strategy in the House is confined to current legislative matters, but their plans reach to 1940—and after. Nothing like them has been seen, or heard, in Congress for many years. They are not the lunatic fringe. They are the Neo-New Dealers.

ROOSEVELT—*And Then?*

Undoubtedly, the moving spirit, guiding genius, and general out-in-front man for this bloc is Maury Maverick. Maverick is a second-term Congressman from San Antonio, Texas. His family name, despite the word of his enemies, did not originate with the cow-country word for unbranded cattle. On the contrary, the word for unbranded cattle originated with his family, specifically with his grandfather who was a pioneer cattleman and, in addition to this venture into nomenclature, was one of the signers of the Texas Declaration of Independence. In the case of the Congressman, at least, the name is descriptive.

How San Antonio, which considers itself somewhat uppercrust among Texas cities, sent Maury Maverick to Congress is something of a mystery. His Texas is the Panhandle or the Big Bend Country, but certainly not San Antonio. He needs a large chair for his body and a large room for his voice. He wears loud shirts and ties which sometimes match. In his office, he works in his shirt-sleeves or with his coat and vest unbuttoned. If his secretary announces a lady caller he slips on his coat or buttons his vest—the two bottom buttons on it. With men he never bothers.

He is a graduate of the Virginia Military Institute and the University of Texas. In one place or the other he must have picked up his share of the social graces. But he never bothers about them either—not the minor ones at least. Washington, which sometimes lionizes the people it most disapproves of, has made some social passes at Maverick. But each time he has seen it coming and ducked. He told me recently that he does not average one dinner out a month while Congress is in session. He takes his work home with him.

Although only twenty-one in 1917, Maverick commanded a company of infantry in the war, was wounded and decorated. He was admitted to the bar at twenty and at twenty-three, a war hero and not yet a radical, he was elected President of the San Antonio Bar Association. His first venture into politics was like all those that followed it. He went in in 1929 as an independent, founded a Citizen's League of reform-minded citizens, fought and defeated the city-county Democratic machine and got out of it, for himself, the undistinguished office of tax collector. But he distinguished himself in it, made friends of all the lower-income citizens and enemies of the higher-income citizens and in 1934 declared for Congress and, to the chagrin of the "First Families" of San Antonio politics, got himself elected.

There was nothing particularly important in the fact that San Antonio sent a Democrat to Congress in 1934. It usually sends Democrats. Maverick, when he came to Washington, was merely another Democratic vote in a Congress that already had more than it needed. His course was marked out for him as it is marked out for all first-term Congressmen. He was expected, as all newcomers are, to make no speeches, vote right and answer his mail. He answered his mail. On the other two items his conduct varied. Usually he voted right. Occasionally he did not. He was ultra-New Deal. He never voted against the party majority except on those few occasions when he thought the party majority was not New Deal enough.

And he did make speeches. Opinions vary on Maverick as a speech-maker. He has very few oratorical tricks. When he has something to say he stands up and hammers it out in a voice that is generally louder than necessary, but with frontier-language of a sort that is too direct to be misunderstood. In the last session his most dramatic speaking forays were on world peace (the peace forces have had no such forceful advocate in the House in many decades), civil liberty, and the activities of various "red baiting" organizations. Before his term was up Maverick had established himself, among radico-liberals throughout the country, as one of their foremost Congressional spokesman. The more orthodox chiefs of the party in Congress were wary of him. His enemies called him a wild man.

San Antonio was not any too well pleased with his reputation. Decades of conventional Congressmen had left it unprepared for Maverick's brand. His enemies got together a sizable war-chest to prevent his renomination. But he won—one version of the story being that Mr. Roosevelt intervened and sent the reluctant party organization to his aid.

At any rate, he is back in Congress, and whatever slight restraints held him in his first term were off in his second. When the President's Supreme Court measure came to the House floor, Maverick, one jump ahead of the leaders, grabbed his copy, got the floor and introduced the bill himself. It was known in the House as the Maverick bill. And Maverick, who is one of the completely enthusiastic supporters of the measure, was immensely pleased. He writes occasional articles for the *Nation* and the *New Republic,* his writing being as monosyllabic and as straightforward as his speaking. He continues to speak frequently at gatherings of liberals. It is a safe guess that the party wheel horses still eye him askance. His continued presence in Congress, is not a portent of peace. But he is very much in the favor of the White House. When the Democratic Victory Dinners were held in Washington early in 1937, the party's top-notch leaders met with the President at $100 a plate. Mr. Farley introduced the President. At a near-by hotel the party proletariat dined with Mrs. Roosevelt at $10 a plate. Mr. Maverick presided and introduced Mrs. Roosevelt.

But Maury Maverick, despite these current occupations, has his eye on the future. He does not believe that the New Deal is primarily emergency legislation. Neither does he believe that all the New Deal has, as yet, been dealt. He thinks that Mr. Roosevelt has started something which will require a good many years

issues he is irreconcilable and a die-hard. He is generally recognized as the leading authority in the House on questions of public power and was co-author, with Senator George Norris, of the administration's bill to create the Tennessee Valley Authority. He managed to get most of northeastern Mississippi tied into the TVA and, in every county of his own district, he has organized county electric power associations and instituted a movement to bring cheap electricity into its rural areas.

Rankin has probably played a lone hand too long and is too much of an individualist to join any hard-and-fast organization of liberals. But he serves as guide, counselor and friend. He watches, with satisfaction, while the younger members disport themselves on a variety of questions. "They are the best thing that has come to Congress in the seventeen years I have been here," he says. "Thanks largely to them there is more individual thinking in the House to-day than at any time since the Civil War." And whenever Congress gets around to the matter of utilities and public power—as it almost always does at every session before adjournment—Rankin, far from being merely an adviser to this bloc, is its leader.

Two other veterans among the Neo-New Dealers are David J. Lewis of Maryland and John A. Martin of Colorado. Lewis, despite the fact that he worked in a coal mine from the age of nine until he was twenty-three, learned to read in a Sunday School and studied Latin with the minister of his church, is one of the scholars of the House. He has been a member of five Congresses. At sixty-eight he is no longer looking for a fight but his liberalism is undiminished. Martin is sixty-nine. He was in Congress for two terms, twenty-five years ago, and came in, again, with the Roosevelt victory in 1932. The available experience of these two men is one reason why the liberal bloc is not likely to go off the deep end.

Another Representative whose Congressional experience antedates the Roosevelt era, and who adds considerable weight to the liberal bloc is Kent Keller of Illinois. Keller—like a noticeable large number of the members of this group—has a remarkable background. His education began in the public schools of Alva, Illinois, and ended with graduate study at Heidelberg, Germany. At one time he taught school. Later he owned and edited a newspaper. He has practiced law. Because of illness he went to Mexico where, for twelve years, he successfully engaged in mining operations. He returned to rural Illinois, went into politics, to quote his own words, "as an aggressive progressive," served in the state Senate and, finally, in 1930, ran for the Congress, overturned the vote in a normally Republican District and, in 1936, was reëlected for the third time. Keller is a student of economics in more than an amateur sense. It is doubtful if anyone in Congress has a better grasp of the problem of unemployment. He is a New Deal Democrat—more New Deal, probably, than Democratic.

In the main, however, the Neo-New Dealers are young—most of them in years, almost all of them in Congressional experience. They came into Congress riding the Roosevelt landslides of 1932, 1934, and 1936. Mr. Roosevelt made them politically possible by making their points of view politically acceptable. Most of them frankly admit the debt, although some of them refuse to be bound, in all matters, to the creditor.

The seven Wisconsin Progressives and the five Farm-Labor Representatives from Minnesota belong in the unbound category. The Wisconsin contingent, among whom Thomas Amlie, Harry Sautoff and Gerald J. Boileau are said to be the most effective, is made up of men most of whom were liberals, under the elder La Follette. They are accustomed to playing lone hands and, I think, rather relish it. With Senator La Follette they meet, every Thursday night, to discuss and determine their stand. On most questions they are whole-hearted supporters of Mr. Roosevelt. But they are decidedly suspicious of the Democratic leadership and are persuaded that the Democratic Party will turn out to be no fit vehicle for the long-run program of the Progressives. A lurking but unexpressed suspicion to the same effect about the Democratic party exists, I think, among others of the Neo-New Dealers. Meanwhile, the Progressives play the game with the liberal Democrats.

The Minnesota Farm-Labor group, along with Lemke and Burdick, Farm-Labor Representatives from

North Dakota, are, in general, left-wing liberals and, like the usual run of radicals, are inclined to make their own laws. Farthest left of them all is John Toussaint Bernard, a war veteran, a miner, and one of the best-read men in Congress, who celebrated his arrival at his first session on the floor by casting the only "no" that was recorded against the government's neutrality policy in regard to Spain. He voted that way to the joy of the Communist "Daily Worker" which promptly ran a long article about him—because he hates Fascism and believes that America's policy of withholding shipments of arms from the loyalist government is helping the Fascists. Despite the fact that Bernard is considerably more radical than the rank-and-file liberals in Congress, he is a coöperative radical; he prefers to go a little distance with the nation than a long way by himself. For that reason he is on more intimate terms with the Neo-New Dealers than some of the other Farm-Labor Representatives.

Among dependable members of Maverick's original group are Mrs. Caroline O'Day of New York, who makes up in hard work and graciousness what she lacks in drama and who, on all questions, can be counted on as a sure-fire liberal; Herman P. Kopplemann of Connecticut whose liberalism flowered and bore fruit in the Connecticut State Senate under the nose of the conservative Republican machine; Charles G. Binderup of Nebraska, a son of Danish homesteaders who went into politics as a side-line to the creamery business and proposes to stay in as a "100 percent farmer-progressive"; E. C. Eicher of Iowa, whose liberalism is bona fide but has to be tempered occasionally to a conservative constituency; Fred Biermann and Otha D. Wearin, also of Iowa; Charles R. Eckert of Pennsylvania; Henry Ellenbogen of Pennsylvania, a labor spokesman; Wright Patman of Texas, who does most of the talking for the liberals on monetary matters.

In geographical distribution and in their coverage of issues the members of the original bloc had contact with every major area of the country and included individuals with some special qualifications on almost every question likely to be a subject for liberal agitation. Having got together in the seventy-fourth Congress, they were prepared for increased coöperation in the seventy-fifth session. What they were quite unprepared for was the large number of recruits that came to Washington in the new Congress, all set, with shining armor, for just such an enterprise.

The shining armor item is not an unimportant one. As Maury Maverick, who is something of a poet, puts it: "they have seen a great light shining." Most of them would undoubtedly refuse to admit any such vision. Nevertheless, their zeal is evangelical and their language—when they talk privately about their plans—is well sprinkled with phrases long dear to the social reformer. The "abundant life" is not a threadbare slogan;

they refer, often, to "future generations of Americans";
mention, frequently, "the under-privileged," "the dispossessed," and, with reverse emphasis, "the money
barons," and "the privileged few." Mr. Roosevelt's
"economic royalists" was meat for their thinking. If
they were young preachers I am sure they would have
a great deal to say about "the kingdom of Heaven." As
it is, they have a firm faith that if we cannot reach
Utopia we can certainly get a good deal closer to it.
They have gone into politics as the best way to prove
that faith with their works.

That, in itself is something out of the ordinary. In
fact, it is difficult to say which is the more unusual: the
fact that they wanted to get into Congress in the first
place or the fact that, having such a desire, they found
voters enough to gratify it. Whatever they are, they are
not run-of-the-mill politicians. But then, as Representative Rankin remarked "the voters don't seem to be
run-of-the-mill voters any more, either."

Undoubtedly there has been a change in what large
sections of the voting public demands of its political
representatives. The change may be only temporary
but while it lasts it is significant. Beginning with the
1932 campaign and continuing through the campaign
of 1936, Mr. Roosevelt has preached and dramatized a
gospel which liberals have cherished, generally in political obscurity, for many years. More than that he has
crossed party lines and brought to the practical, ballot-

box support of that gospel a great mass of hitherto inarticulate voters. These young Congressmen would
probably have believed as they do even though there
had been no Mr. Roosevelt and no New Deal. But they
would not have been Congressmen. A chief reason,
therefore, why they are in politics is because now, for
the first time, they can take their particular kind of convictions into politics with a fair chance that they will get
somewhere.

Since, save for the Farm-Labor and Wisconsin Progressive groups, all of them are Democrats, their arrival
is timely. Particularly in the North where the influence
of the city machines has been largely dominant, the
Democratic Party has needed an infusion of intellectual
respectability. These newcomers would deny that they
were an asset in that direction and some of the orthodox
party leaders would probably agree with them. Nevertheless, among the genuinely liberal Democrats who
take a long look at the party's future there is a great
deal of satisfaction that they have arrived.

It is generally agreed, I think, that one of the likeliest of the newcomers is Jerry Voorhis of California,
thirty-six years old, a Democrat and a school teacher.
Maury Maverick found Voorhis soon after the seventy-
fifth Congress convened. There is no similarity in the
personalities of the two men, but they hit it off at once.
With Maverick's help he has already moved well to the
front among the Neo-New Dealers.

Voorhis graduated from Yale in 1923 with Phi Beta Kappa. He returned to California, got his Master's degree from Claremont College, spent several years knocking around the West at a variety of odd jobs and finally settled down as headmaster of a private school which his father had established for under-privileged boys. He is a lay reader in the Episcopal Church and takes his religion seriously. He has three hobbies: boys, baseball, and American history—and has had considerable success at all three of them. He has plenty of money, wears old clothes, smokes a straight-stem pipe, talks more like Harvard than Yale, seldom makes speeches but is an excellent speaker and never ran for public office in his life until 1936 when he won his Congressional seat by a Democratic majority which was large even in a Roosevelt election. Already he is being urged to run for governor of California in 1938. To date, he has not been tempted.

Until the New Deal appeared, Voorhis was a registered Socialist. "That," he told me, "was the only way I could vote my protest against the reactionary leadership of both major parties. I was never a full-fledged Socialist and now Mr. Roosevelt has made it possible for me to be a Democrat with a clear conscience."

A number of other Congressional newcomers have established a considerable influence in this liberal bloc. Robert C. Allen of Pennsylvania is one of them. Allen is 35, a graduate of Phillips-Andover Academy and

Harvard. He is a successful manufacturer. Norman R. Hamilton of Virginia is a newspaper owner and an older man. The state machine of Virginia, controlled by Senator Byrd, was much too lukewarm on the New Deal to suit Hamilton. As a result he declared war on the machine in his district in the last election and defeated it. W. J. Fitzgerald and A. N. Phillips, Jr., are anti-utility, pro-labor liberals from previously Republican districts in Connecticut. Frank W. Fries is a former miner and a mine owner from the Springfield district in Illinois which sent Abraham Lincoln to the House.

Now the bloc of which these members are representative is not organized in any formal sense. Meetings, however, are rather frequent and usually prolonged into the night. Maverick generally calls the members together. The agenda is usually limited to a consideration of some specific legislation that is pending or in prospect. When the occasion calls for it, an outline is drawn up of the kind of legislation the members of the bloc desire, their names are signed and the statement presented on the floor of the House. It is significant that, in their declarations, the Neo-New Dealers generally desire to go further than the New Deal administration, to date, has shown itself willing to go.

In these activities, however, there is nothing to offend the party leaders in Congress or give them any outright cause for alarm. Members of Congress have got together and petitioned the House on all sorts of subjects from time immemorial. The fact that these proposals may be somewhat advanced, is not regarded as insubordination. After all, on most issues, most of the members of the bloc are politically well-behaved; up to the present they have upset no important applecarts; they know their places and they get to them in time to vote, when voting is necessary. From the standpoint of the party wheel horses, they probably take their politics too seriously and skirt the edges of too many explosive questions. But the chances are that—their good behavior on vital matters having been established—most of them will deserve and get the party's reëlection blessing in 1938.

That blessing, whatever it proves about the party chieftains, will indicate the political astuteness of the Neo-New Dealers. The first point in their strategy— and the place where they differ most widely from previous liberal groups—is their willingness to go slow. The few left-wing members, like Bernard, who are likely to act as they think and risk the consequences are more than off-set by the majority who value their political necks, know how easy it is to lose them and realize how ineffective they would be once their necks were lost.

One of the veteran conservatives in Congress admitted, ruefully, to me that there was enough ability and courage in this up-start bloc to keep the country in a state of legislative ferment for a good many sessions to come. I do not believe that there is any immediate basis for such a fear. Ferment is not a part of the immediate strategy of the group. Between now and 1940 the New Deal, First and Second, will probably be ferment enough to satisfy them. Meanwhile, a good many of the new members among them will have had time to build political fences back home substantial enough, perhaps, to survive an election in which Mr. Roosevelt does not head the ticket.

Moreover, this one-thing-at-a-time strategy has been accepted for another reason. There is no doubt that most of them could get together now on a long-time program. But to attempt to do that, in the opinion of such men as Maverick and Voorhis, would be to get the cart before the horse. The immediate job, as they regard it, is to prove that they can agree and hold together on current legislative matters. That is not always easy, particularly in view of the fact that reformers are notably impatient and these particular reformers have a full quota of prima donnas among them. The Farmer-Laborites are not notably good coöperators. Some of the Wisconsin Progressives are inclined to regard themselves as the Chosen Liberals. Maury Maverick, who seldom handles people with gloves, has aroused some slight irritation and some jealousy. For the time being, therefore, a long-time program can be held in abeyance while the members of the bloc get on solid ground with each other in regard to less ambitious undertakings.

And they are shrewd enough to know that, in the matter of long-time programs, the country has just about reached the saturation point. They will be satisfied to help along the process of absorption.

This insistence upon coöperation which, in itself, is something new among Congressional liberals, is likely to produce results not only because the strategy of the group is to go slow, but also because the members of the group are not doctrinaires. Congress has had a good many lone-wolf liberals and has been able, generally, to take them in its stride largely because they have been attached to certain pet theories which they were unwilling to modify until this new bloc appeared. There has been nothing approaching a united liberal front since the elder La Follette was in the House forty years ago. This new generation, however, is not interested in theories and is not alarmed at labels. It wants results. "We haven't any preconceived ideas," says Voorhis, "as to where America will be going twenty years from now. We want to insure today's progress. If we were to divide into different schools of thought our time would be spent debating our philosophies and we'd get exactly nowhere."

I asked Voorhis whether there were any Communists in the group.

"I don't know," he said, "I've never taken the trouble to find out. I do know that the one thing we'd probably turn thumbs down on quicker than anything else would be a discussion of Communism or, for that matter, of Socialism or Capitalism. There's too much to do."

It is obvious, however, that such a bloc as this could never have come into existence except for a fundamental likemindedness among its members. Their discussions and their joint declarations are largely limited to current legislation. But, with individual variations, very much the same ideas are in the backs of the minds of most of them. And most of them know it. That is why, even when the arguments wax hot, the atmosphere of their meetings is congenial. They argue on most current issues but, more important than that, they are in general agreement on more fundamental matters even though, to date, they have not found it expedient to say so.

With one or two exceptions, they agree, I think, in their belief in our private profit economy. To conservatives they undoubtedly sound like Socialists. Outside office hours some of them are apt to be found in Socialist company. But they are not Socialists. They will agree with anyone that capitalism needs to have a lot done to it but they are at least proceeding on the assumption that the repairs can be made and that—repaired—a capitalistic system probably has more to offer than any of the available alternatives. And if it turns out that the system has to be scrapped, they want the scrapping done by an evolutionary process.

Their idea of repairing, however, is radical. Without any exceptions that I could find, they refuse to regard the New Deal either as an emergency undertaking or a finished job. One of them who said he had enough to answer for already and refused to be quoted declared to me that "we do not believe our system is necessarily safe or fundamentally healthy merely because it has recovered. Our restoratives have worked. But we haven't done very much, as yet, about the disease."

Doing something about the disease involves, for most of them, a good many things. It certainly involves a continued attack on the utilities and a greatly extended public power program. On this in fact they are miniature George Norrises. Some of them would have a little TVA on every river of any size in America: "abundant power, at a low price, in every home." A few of them would extend this nationalization principle to coal—"a basic commodity and a sick industry."

I think that a majority would agree, also, that the last legislative word has by no means been spoken on the matter of banking and monetary reform. The joint statement which the bloc may issue on this question and for which the preliminary research is already under way may call upon the government to take the Federal Reserve System out of private hands and nationalize it under a Federal Monetary Authority.

They appear to have no very great enthusiasm for crop-curtailment as a permanent cure for the ills of agriculture. They are convinced, however, that most of those ills can be cured and that the most likely way to do it is, again, by government intervention—with the government, in this case, reviving in modified form the plan of the McNary-Haugen bill to regulate prices by buying the farmers' surplus and storing it against domestic shortage or selling it abroad. They are for more drastic efforts to decrease farm tenancy by government purchase and resale.

It is safe to say that all of them are pro-labor. If the issue of the sit-down strike came to a vote in the House most of the members of this bloc would refuse to condemn it. They want collective bargaining made the indisputable law of the land and minimum wages and maximum hours fixed by Congressional legislation. Their public statement on a long-time program for the unemployed leaned heavily to the Icke's view of Public Works—and additional large expenditures—rather than to the made-work program of Mr. Hopkins. To pay the bill, their proposals advocate less borrowing and higher taxes particularly, I gather, on the earnings of the substantial income groups. So far as I could discover there is no great alarm among them as yet over the unbalanced state of the Federal budget. "It will cost a lot of money," one of them said, "but what the hell is money where lives are involved."

That, incidentally, is not a bad summation of the basic philosophy of the entire group. They are not financially irresponsible. It is true that a few of them—particularly several members from the state of Washington—are more than casually inclined toward Townsendism. But some of them, on the other hand, were obliged to win their seats against the opposition of the Townsend organization. The important point is that their opinions on questions of finance are a product of their attitude toward society. In regard to the social order—present and future—they are humanitarians—with no apologies to offer to anyone. They actually believe that the United States is potentially rich enough to make it possible for all its citizens to live at a comfortable economic level and to be made secure against want. They do not think that the establishment of that standard of living and security can safely be left to chance, to natural law or to the voluntary good will of private citizens. They are for Mr. Roosevelt because they regard his New Deal as the first significant and inclusive effort to do, by legislation, what they do not believe can be accomplished any other way. They are certain that the only way to save the system—or, for that matter to make the system worth saving—is to finish the job.

Some of them were concerned, before Congress convened, lest the reëlected Mr. Roosevelt would call a halt to this effort. Their concern has been largely dispelled. Up to the present, the President, in most matters, has been a step or two ahead of them. Their anxiety now has been transferred to 1940 and the post-

Roosevelt period. If they survive the 1938 elections they will have a hand in determining the 1940 liberal and Democratic strategy. No other group in Congress will be in such an excellent position to serve as the emissaries for organized labor and organized agriculture. The presence of a majority of them in the counsels of the Democratic Party may help to prevent the emergence, in that election, of a Third Party. On the other hand, most of them are more liberal than Democratic and if the 1940 candidate and platform are not in the Roosevelt-New Deal tradition they may very well desert the Democrats for a third party that will be more dependably liberal.

Meanwhile, they will continue to keep their spurs polished; do their heavy thinking in solitude and their heavy fighting as a group; play some politics for re-election purposes; be less respectful, if reëlected, to their political superiors; and long before 1940 have hammered out a Neo-New Deal program that will give the Democratic Party a chance to separate, once and for all, its liberal sheep from its conservative goats.

CHAPTER XI

WHERE DO THE DEMOCRATS GO FROM HERE?

During Franklin D. Roosevelt's first administration the New Deal was looked upon, and hated or embraced, as an economic phenomenon. It was the body economic and not the body politic that was being operated on. If anything untoward was happening to the body politic it was good Democratic strategy to conceal the fact.

The political consequences of the New Deal, to be sure, were much written about and warned against. But the President and Mr. Farley were far too effective peacemakers to allow those consequences to be made an issue. They were not an issue in the 1936 election even after the defection of such notable Democrats as Alfred E. Smith and John W. Davis and the silence of such others as Newton D. Baker and Owen D. Young. The average American voter wanted economic salvation. The average Democratic politician wanted to win. The

President and his program brought those two desires into happy union and the result was a landslide.

But the union was one of convenience and is not likely to endure. Those whose first article of faith is the Democratic party are ready to ease out the economic salvationists and their plans of salvation and restore, again, the inoffensive Democracy with which they were familiar in the traditional era before Mr. Roosevelt. Those, on the other hand, whose political passions are centered wholly on economic issues, have no particular devotion to the Democratic party save in so far as they can use it as the vehicle for their liberalism. The issue, therefore, is to determine whether the Democratic party is to be the Democratic party as it has always been or whether it is now to become the liberal party. Party history and a powerful coterie of party leaders are on the side of a return to tradition. The legislative record of the New Deal and—obviously—the President are on the side of the liberals.

The result of this conflict will certainly determine the choice of the Democratic candidate in 1940, seriously affect the party's prospects in that year, determine the fate of the Third Party movement and have a direct bearing upon the long-time status of the Roosevelt program and the place in history of Mr. Roosevelt.

To understand the attitude of the traditional Democrat in this controversy it is necessary to recall the constituency of the Democratic Party and the position to which, for many decades, it has been committed.

In any normal political season the composition of the Democratic Party is easily definable. It has two chief elements in it. The first is southern, with the twelve states of the solid South whose sure-fire electoral votes have been enough to keep Democratic hopes alive in even the most hopelessly Republican years. In these, and the somewhat less Democratic states of the border, the Democratic tradition has its roots in the slavery issue, the Civil War and reconstruction. Nowhere else is American politics so undilutedly Bourbon and so unashamedly reactionary.

It is true, that, recently, the South has produced a few political leaders who are notable exceptions to the run-of-the-mill. Senator now Justice Hugo Black of Alabama, for instance, is—by the conventional southern standards—more a New Dealer than a Democrat.

Senator "Jimmy" Byrnes of South Carolina is another liberal. So is Senator Claude Pepper of Florida. So, also, is Maury Maverick—insurgent Representative from San Antonio, Texas. There are others. But their presence in Congress, whatever it proves, does not prove that southern Democracy has seen the liberal light and is about to embrace the new gospel. The authentic spokesmen for Southern Democracy are such men as Senators Byrd and Glass of Virginia, Harrison of Mississippi, Smith of South Carolina, George of Georgia, and Overton of Louisiana. Their school is the old school. By and large, the solid South wants no other.

The second major element of Democratic strength comes from the cities of the North and particularly the Northeast. The men who run the machines which garner these city votes are not driven by their devotion to any particular national issues. New York's Tammany Hall and Boston's Curley and Hurley machines, the Kelly organization in Chicago and the miniature Tammany of "Boss" Prendegast in Kansas City are not in politics because of the issues but because of the spoils. Save where the spoils system is involved it is a part of their strength that they stand for nothing in particular. Their aim is to deliver the vote—which they do.

On the surface at least, no two political groups could be farther apart than these city machines and the solid South. The background of the first is industrial and proletarian. The background of the second is agricultural and aristocratic. The southern politician still uses oratory on his constituents and puts his faith in principles —generally with a strong Scriptural flavoring. The city politician has long since substituted a card file and a system of rewards and punishments for oratory and looks upon principles as the luxury of those who are not obliged to make politics pay.

When it comes to practical politics, however, they both talk the same language. In the preaching and the practice of party regularity they are blood brothers. A straight ticket means the same thing in New York City as in Alabama; a split-ticket voter is as much to be shunned or coerced in the one place as in the other. In both places unquestioning party obedience is enforced with the same rigidity. Any development which makes that enforcement more difficult is looked upon as a threat to the strength of these organizations and sooner or later is certain to feel the weight of their combined opposition.

It has been chiefly from those two sources—the South and the Northeast—that the Democrats have recruited their strength. It has been the South, however, which, in national politics, has provided the party with its dominant point of view. The major interest of the city machines has been local—that is city and state affairs. Their organizations and their leadership have been geared to operate in that area. They have been content to leave the party's national policies very largely in the hands of the southern Democrats. Thus, until the advent of Mr. Roosevelt, it was Jack Garner or the late Joe Robinson or Pat Harrison or Carter Glass who spoke out for the party on national affairs.

The point of view which was fastened upon the party by the Democrats of the South was, to put it mildly, conservative. It was a conservatism that had its roots in a firm devotion to the principle of State's rights—a principle that gave ample ground from which to oppose all manner of liberalizing and regulatory economic

legislation. It was a conservatism that had as its background the quasi-feudal system that prevails in many
parts of the South. It was a conservatism, too, that was
acutely conscious of the enlarged economic opportunities which the continuance of that system seemed to
promise in view of the increasing number of industrialists who, seeking escape from the consequences of liberal economic legislation in the northern states, were
moving their plants south. State's rights conservatism
had begun to pay. The wheel horse Democratic leaders
saw to it that no national commitments were fastened
on the party which would threaten the dividends.

It is true that the Republican Party, meanwhile, had
established itself as the official voice of conservatism
and that, on almost all really fundamental issues, there
were no important differences between Republicans and
Democrats. The Democrats, of course, were in the opposition. For that reason they were obliged, every now
and again, to give some evidence of disagreement. But
the opposition was not very authentic. I do not recall
that, during the period between the World War and
Mr. Roosevelt, the effective liberals in Congress had
a single southern Democrat among them. The effective
liberals were such undependable Republicans as George
Norris and Robert M. La Follette.

The late Senator Thomas J. Walsh of Montana was
a liberal and a Democrat. But no one will maintain, I
think, that Senator Walsh's position was representa-

tive of any considerable number of his party associates from the South. Senator Burton K. Wheeler, also of Montana, was—and is—likewise a liberal. But just how much his liberalism was at home in the Democratic party in the pre-Roosevelt days is indicated by his 1924 campaign for the Vice-Presidency on the third-party ticket with the elder La Follette. In short, the point of view of such intransigent Democratic Senators as Walsh and Wheeler was no more abhorrent to the Republicans than to the southern Democrats.

The southern Democrats, who had begun to accept their dominance in the party's national councils as something fixed and permanent, have suffered no end of inner torment during these last, presumably triumphant, Democratic years. It has been plain to them that Mr. Roosevelt had very little in common with either their philosophy or their program. George Norris and Bob La Follette were more congenial to his mind than Jack Garner or Pat Harrison. The President scrupulously observed the political amenities of the party. But he persistently did violence to what had been its political and economic position.

From the traditional Democratic point of view both the origin and the administration of the President's program have been alien. The policies he initiated were a direct blow at the state's-rights conservatism of the Democracy of the South. The manner in which those policies have been administered is an equally serious threat to the system of rigid party regularity by which the Democratic organizations, in both the South and the Northeast, built up and maintained their strength.

The platform on which Mr. Roosevelt was elected in 1932 departed in many particulars from the conventional Democratic platforms of previous years. But it was not a New Deal platform. Mr. Roosevelt's 1932 campaign, however, went far beyond the platform. It was a New Deal campaign. In it he confessed an economic point of view and outlined a program of economic reform which the stalwarts at the Chicago convention never intended and probably would not have endorsed.

But they did not complain—not openly. The party, after so many lean years, appeared to be on the road to victory. Party unity had to be preserved and was. Those who sufficiently understood what Mr. Roosevelt was driving at to be alarmed doubtless comforted themselves with the thought that a candidate on campaign was a very different person than a President in office.

In this they reckoned without two facts, one of which should have been a warning to them. They failed, first of all, to appraise Mr. Roosevelt correctly. Their estimate of him at Chicago was of a man with a vote-getting name and personality who had served two terms as governor of a state whose electoral votes were necessary to a Democratic victory. If, contrary to convention procedure, they had taken time to dig a bit into his record, both in the New York Senate and as governor, they would have found adequate basis for the misgivings which, too late, materialized.

They would have found that the economic liberalism which cropped out in the New Deal was not something assumed for campaign purposes. Mr. Roosevelt had consistently stood with the liberals ever since, as a youthful State Senator, he had taken the lead in the fight against the traction interests. They would have been warned by the independence of a Democrat who once boasted that, in thirty years of voting, he had split his ticket every year save one, and whose political strength in his own state was derived, in part at least, from the readiness with which he took issue with the state and particularly the New York City Democratic machines. There was very little in his record to please either the state's rights conservatives or the apostles of party regularity.

But there was no such investigation. Mr. Roosevelt was nominated. He flew to Chicago to accept the nomination. The delegates cheered what they called his courage—meaning chiefly by that his untraditional personal appearance and his declaration against prohibition. It was not until they were safely home again and the Roosevelt campaign well under way that they awoke to the unpleasant discovery of how much more Mr. Roosevelt had declared for in his acceptance speech than repeal and how—as his campaign unfolded—he was committing them and their party to a point of view which, if it was not exactly new, was certainly not Democratic as the dominant party leaders understood and defined it.

But this discovery, as I have said, did not injure the party's unity. No Democrats of importance "took a walk." Those who had their doubts continued to bank heartily on "the sobering effects of the Presidency" and, sensing victory, went along with the candidate.

Before Mr. Roosevelt's first inauguration, however, another fact appeared to upset the calculations of those who hoped that the Roosevelt liberalism was merely emotional and the New Deal only a campaign slogan. By the fourth of March 1933, the economic crisis had grown so acute that even the most hesitant of the party's conservatives agreed as to the need for drastic action. Mr. Roosevelt acted—drastically and with dispatch. Because every one was badly frightened, both Congress and the country declared a moratorium on criticism. In the N.R.A., the A.A.A. and a long list of other measures the New Deal was made the law of the land. Under the protection of the emergency, liberalism was entrenched.

Some of Mr. Roosevelt's critics believe that if there had been no emergency there would have been no New Deal. That conclusion, again, is a result of an inadequate appraisal of Mr. Roosevelt. I am sure that, in some form or other, all the permanent legislation which was passed in his first administration was always on his agenda. The measures which were enacted during 1933 and 1934 were not only his program for recovery. They were an expression of his economic philosophy. The fact of the emergency influenced the shaping of the legislation just as that fact speeded its passage. But in none of these measures was the President in the position of a man who is obliged, by the exigencies of a situation, to endorse a course of procedure of which, at heart, he does not approve. On the contrary, the situation only served to facilitate the speedier accomplishment of policies which he had always stood for. And even with the aid of the emergency, his first four years in office did not, by any means, complete the economic reforms which he believes to be desirable. That is plain from the even more drastic measures of the Second New Deal with which he launched his second term.

But the significant fact here is that the liberal legislation of Mr. Roosevelt's first administration did not reflect the point of view of the party's leaders. It reflected the point of view of Franklin D. Roosevelt and of a strange circle of counselors, who, whatever else they were, were certainly not acceptable Democrats. The party leaders complained that they were called in only when it was necessary to have their signatures at the bottom of the page to make the document legal.

The seriousness of the crisis probably was a good excuse for some reasonable measure of nonpartisanship. But the President carried nonpartisanship far beyond that point. He carried it, in fact, beyond politics altogether. That was resented almost as much by the Republicans as by the Democrats.

Mr. Roosevelt's advisers—the most intimate of them —were political unknowns. Their records—as they appeared to the party leaders—were not of a sort to inspire confidence in the "soundness" of their advice or to give comfort to those who believed that the maintenance of the party organization must be the first concern of the politician. Some of them were experts, most of them had brains, few of them were out to get anything for themselves. But all of them had a zeal for the job and a scorn for the political consequences.

Perhaps the measures which constituted the First New Deal would never have been passed if the President had followed the customary political procedure and confined his consultations to the party leaders and such political laymen as the party leaders would have approved of. He did not follow that procedure. If the Democrats on Capitol Hill have any pride in the New Deal it is certainly not the pride of authorship. Its authorship goes back to the President, himself, and to the assortment of political hybrids with which he was surrounded.

Moreover, the administration of the New Deal was no more Democratic than its authorship. All down the line, whenever the administration of a particular measure has involved New Deal objectives, administrative authority has been kept out of the hands of the Demo-

cratic politicians and given to individuals whose qualifications, whatever they were, were not political.

The first two years of Mr. Roosevelt's first administration were the heyday of the Brain Trust—of many
Brain Trusts. While Ray Moley and Rex Tugwell and
Adolph Berle, rank outsiders, hovered around the White
House, lesser Moleys and Tugwells and Berles moved
into the various departments and sat next to the places
of authority. Washington was aswarm with strange
people: young men who smoked pipes and rolled up
their sleeves to make America over; and young women
who smoked cigarettes at their office desks, discussed
economic trends in their boarding houses, were cynical of
all that had gone before and starry-eyed about all that
was about to be. Nothing like this had ever before been
seen in the history of American politics. And whatever
this was it was not politics—not as Washington or the
Democratic party had understood and practiced it.

In the higher administrative posts the situation, from
the standpoint of the party leaders, was just as bad. The
New Deal for agriculture has been administered by
Henry A. Wallace, a former Republican too liberal for
his party. The New Deal for industry and labor was entrusted to General Hugh A. Johnson who may be a
Democrat but whose partisanship is notable chiefly because of his friendship for Bernard Baruch. After General Johnson came Donald R. Richburg, a progressive
Chicago labor lawyer who, prior to his association with

the present administration, is not known to have ever lifted a finger on behalf of the Democracy. The New Deal for the unemployed has been in the hands of Harry Hopkins and Harold Ickes. Mr. Hopkins had been a social worker in New York City. Mr. Ickes, a Theodore Roosevelt Progressive, has been a supporter of many political lost causes in Chicago—all of them aimed to embarrass, not to assist, the local politicians.

The New Deal for Wall Street, the chairmanship of the Securities Exchange Commission, was first committed to Joseph B. Kennedy, a man with Wall Street experience who would not, however, have qualified as the Wall Street candidate for the job. Later the SEC was presided over by James Landis, a Frankfurter lawyer. The New Deal for the Tennessee Valley, the Tennessee Valley Authority, is jointly administered by David Lilienthal and Dr. Arthur E. Morgan—the former a liberal Wisconsin lawyer and the latter an engineer and former president of Antioch College. The New Deal for the aged and for to-morrow's unemployed, provided for under the Social Security Act, was first put in the hands of John G. Winant, a former Republican Governor of New Hampshire who was notably out of step with the leadership of either his own or the Democratic party. Governor Winant resigned in the 1936 campaign in order to answer the attacks of his one-time Republican colleagues on the Social Security Law.

Only in the Reconstruction Finance Corporation, a

Hoover hang-over, has a major New Deal activity been controlled by an entirely acceptable Democrat. There Jesse Jones, appointed first by Mr. Hoover, still carries on. But he has been surrounded by a group of young and liberal intellectuals who are an adequate foil for his political orthodoxy.

Thus the liberals, having entrenched their ideas in the New Deal legislation were found entrenched in the administration of that legislation. This was a threat both to the conservatism of the solid South and to the integrity of the party machines in both the South and the Northeast where, in the matter of jobs as well as of voting, the enforcement of party regularity was always the primary consideration.

This condition of internal unhappiness was not helped any by the conduct of the 1936 campaign. Nationally, every reasonable effort was made to make it clear that that campaign was not, essentially, a party undertaking. Party propaganda was carefully kept out of all campaign literature. Except for the campaign handbook, prepared for local party workers, there was scarcely any reference to the achievements of the Democratic party, as a party, in all the innumerable folders, leaflets, and pamphlets produced by Charlie Michelson's publicity department.

When it came to the costly business of radio campaigning, the most frequently featured speakers were not the well-known party orators. It is true that on one occasion six Democratic governors were put on the air in a single broadcast. But they were chosen, not because they were Democrats but because, like Mr. Landon, they were governors. The hardest hitting radio campaigner of them all was Harold Ickes, with General Hugh Johnson a close second. The Vice-Presidential candidate, Mr. Garner, was heard but once; the Senate leader, Mr. Robinson, not much more than that. Mr. Homer Cummings, the Attorney-General, was a former chairman of the Democratic National Committee. He was not a major campaign figure. Mr. Farley, reversing his earlier tactics and observing those of John Hamilton, lapsed into a silence early in the campaign which was hardly broken until election night.

I do not believe that the President, himself, mentioned the party by name more than three times in the entire campaign. He did not mention the Republican Party at all or refer, even indirectly, to the Republican candidate. On one occasion he visited Democratic National Headquarters in New York City. On another occasion he summoned a large group of party wheel horses to Hyde Park for a consultation which was as much social as political. Aside from those two gestures and the fact that his opening campaign speech was made at the New York State Democratic convention he did his campaigning, not as a Democrat, but as a New Deal liberal fighting not for party success but for a cause.

There was more to this departure from conventional partisan practice than appeared in the content of the

President's speeches. In Minnesota, Mr. Roosevelt threw his support to the Farmer-Labor ticket and the Democrats were eliminated altogether. In Wisconsin his aid and comfort were extended to the La Follette Progressive party rather than to the regular Democratic candidates and the La Follettes won. In Nebraska his outspoken support brought about the reëlection of Senator George Norris and the upset of the well-laid plans of Arthur Mullen's Omaha Tammany—the official Democratic organization. In Massachusetts, although Governor Curley, aspiring to the Senate, sought desperately to attach himself to the Roosevelt band-wagon, the President carefully avoided anything which might have been construed as a Curley endorsement—a fact which was immediately interpreted—and probably correctly—as a Curley repudiation. In New York City, while Mr. Farley labored to keep Tammany in line, the President looked with favor upon the political activities of the American Labor Party which were certainly a potential threat to Tammany. So far as the solid South was concerned, trouble was laid up for the party by the open and unprecedented Democratic drive to win the support of the northern Negroes.

Certainly no Democratic campaign had ever before been conducted like this. It no more reflected the traditional Democratic ideas of electioneering, than the origin and administration of the New Deal reflected its traditional ideas of government. The old-line Democrats went along with the President and the New Deal because they bore a Democratic label. The liberals went along with the Democratic party because it bore a New Deal label. Neither was particularly happy in the company of the other. The old-line Democrats looked upon the liberals as interlopers. The liberals looked upon the old-line Democrats as opportunists. For election purposes, since they both wanted to win, they managed to get along together. The product of their union was the 1936 landslide.

It is exceedingly improbable that they can be held together long enough to produce another—either in 1938 or in 1940. The Democratic party may win in both elections. It has the momentum. Moreover, it still has Mr. Roosevelt and with due allowance for his Supreme Court set-back, Mr. Roosevelt is undoubtedly still the nation's greatest vote-getter.

Mr. Farley who built and ran the machinery of the 1936 victory believes that there has been a permanent shift in the party alignment of the nation's voters, and that the Democrats have at last become the majority party. He confidently looks forward to fifty years of Democratic fatness—with the Republicans as undernourished as the Democrats were during the half century after Lincoln. His optimism is based upon the greatly increased Democratic registration in every northern state and particularly in such important states as Pennsylvania, California, Illinois, and Massachusetts. But Mr.

Farley—a perennial optimist and proponent of party peace—leaves out of account the rapidly emerging issue as to what and whose the Democratic party is to be; whether it is to be Mr. Roosevelt's kind of a Democratic party with his kind of leaders or whether it is to be, once more, the Democratic party of the pre-Roosevelt period with the pre-Roosevelt leaders back in the saddle. The determination of that issue is likely to have far more to do with the party's vote in 1940 than the increase in Democratic registration.

The old-line leaders of the party one meets in Washington and elsewhere are pretty sure of themselves. They believe that they can safely begin at once the work of dismantling the New Deal and demobilizing the New Dealers. They are convinced that by 1940 that job can be well on toward completion and the Democratic party made, again, a party in which Carter Glass and Jack Garner and even Al Smith and Jim Reed and John W. Davis would feel perfectly at home. In the long run they would rather lose with that kind of a Democracy than win with any other. They understand it. They know how to run it. Up to 1932 they did run it. Moreover, that kind of a Democracy expresses their most cherished economic and political convictions—which the liberal Democracy of the New Deal certainly does not do.

It seems probable that the engineer of this movement of restoration will be the Vice-President, Mr. Garner.

During the first four years Mr. Garner went along with the New Deal like a "good soldier"—if a somewhat silent one. But it is doubtful if any Democrat of importance who has gone along has been less of a New Dealer than the Vice-President. I do not mean, by that, that he has not been for many of the New Deal's measures. During the first four years he was probably for most of them. He had been for some of them—higher taxes in the upper brackets, more stringent utility regulations, better banking laws—since long before the New Deal.

I do not mean, either, that he has hesitated when he did not agree. In regard to some points in the early Roosevelt program he was unquestionably a doubter. But not by so much as the crook of a finger did he ever let his doubts get the better of him. Not in public, at least.

Mr. Garner was not indispensable to the New Deal in that first period. Neither was he a liability. He was what he had been elected to be—a Vice-President, as circumspect and, to all appearances, as impotent as dozens of Vice-Presidents had been before him. It is no discredit to the New Dealers that they did not anticipate events and try to make him feel at home in the New Deal camp. Their energies were employed, as they would have explained, with people that mattered, converting some and cracking down on others. But even though they had tried Mr. Garner could never have been made to feel at home in their camp. By temperament, if not by conviction, he was separated by a vast gulf from the army in which he served.

First of all, of course, Mr. Garner is a Democrat. He believes that the party is bigger than John Garner or any other man and that it is more important than this or any other administration. He likes the company of good fellows. But he particularly likes the company of good Democrats.

The New Deal was strange to him and stranger still were many of the New Dealers. There were few Democrats of standing in all the upper reaches of the new administration. He had been in Congress thirty-five years and he has a flair for remembering faces. But the faces he saw at the New Deal's counsel tables were as unfamiliar as some of the ideas he heard expressed there. This— whatever it was—was not congenial company.

Furthermore, Mr. Garner does not belong to the intelligentsia and he makes no bones about it. He once asked a bright young member of Congress: "who in hell is Herodotus" and left the explaining Congress to wonder whether he really wanted to know or merely wished to flaunt his lack of learning. The Congressional Record is his only heavy reading. He reads it every morning, from cover to cover. He is ambitious, but no crusader. The World War was the first and, so far as I know, the only occasion on which the flaming torch made any appeal to him.

Moreover, John Garner is a success story in the conventional and more recently repudiated American tradition. In his youth his father staked him to the gift of a mule. By dint of shrewd trading and frugality he turned that mule into a fortune. He went to West Texas to build up his health. He built it up, got himself elected to the Texas Legislature, persuaded the legislators to carve out a new Congressional District in his home territory along the Rio Grande and persuaded the voters of the New District to make him their Representative. In Congress, by the practice of nothing more spectacular than honesty, regularity, and good fellowship, and helped along by the inexorable operation of the rule of seniority he rose to the chairmanship of the Committee of Ways and Means. He eventually became floor leader and Speaker of the House. His closest friends say that he never believed, in 1932, that he had a chance for the Presidency. But he was, at least, among those considered. With such a record, unlighted at any point by a glimmer of heterodoxy, it was inevitable that the New Dealers should put him down as one of that presumably superannuated company known as the Old Guard and conclude that, in the quiet backwaters of the Vice-Presidency, he could safely be ignored.

In this, of course, the New Dealers erred. They erred in believing that either the Vice-President or the Old Guard could be ignored. The Old Guard was too numerous and the Vice-President too influential. When the New Deal came to Washington, Mr. Garner had thirty-five years on Capitol Hill to his credit. His influence was partly a result of that long service. In part, however, it was compounded out of certain intangible, but highly regarded qualities: his unfailing friendliness, his love for a fight and his abhorrence of grudges, his honesty and, in all matters of importance to the party, his regularity. His hold on the party in Congress was such that —even in their heyday—the New Dealers blundered when they left him out of their reckonings.

Whether or not Mr. Garner welcomed the restful status to which he was consigned, there is no doubt that during the first New Deal he meticulously observed it. Shortly after the New Deal took over, the late Tom Heflin remarked: "Jack Garner will make a good Vice-President. He'll never have to apologize for anything. All he'll have to say will be 'when did I ever say that?' " As floor leader in the House he had been an unfailing source of news. As Vice-President he kept up his friendship with the newspaper men. But he told them nothing. He still tells them nothing. "I'm as clear of news," he says, "as the waters of the Leona River." When several months ago, he emerged from a protracted luncheon conference with the President, the White House correspondents cornered him and insisted that something of importance must have been under discussion. "No," he said, "it was just one of those fancy lunches and I had trouble with the peas."

But Mr. Garner's reticence as Vice-President does not

mean that he has lost any of his influence with Congress. On the contrary, as the First and Second New Deals unfolded his influence perceptibly increased. His office more and more became a haven of refuge for bewildered Congressmen. If he had no cure for their troubles, he was at least a sympathetic listener. In the midst of so much unsettlement the Vice-President was a fixture. A Senator emerging from his office one day nodded toward the door and remarked to a friend: "Jack Garner! There he stands." A great many men feel that way about him. It was clear long before the Court fight, that in any break between the old-line Democrats and the President, Mr. Garner's influence—if he chose to exert it— would be a decisive factor.

Meanwhile, all the evidence indicates that the stage is set for a political realignment. I believe that the stage was set deliberately and not by chance. The President is too adept at the business of politics to be unaware of the consequences to the party of the course he has pursued.

He is convinced that the two-party system is meaningless unless there is some fundamental difference in the philosophy and the aims of the two parties. He does not believe that the Republican Party will ever be anything other than the conservative party. He knows that policies of the sort incorporated in the First and Second New Deal will not be safe for long if their future is left to the mercy of a Democratic party with the pre-Roosevelt leadership and the pre-Roosevelt point of view. I am sure that he does not propose to leave them there.

CHAPTER XII

WHERE DOES MR. ROOSEVELT GO FROM HERE?

WHEN Jim Farley, following the administration's defeat on the Supreme Court measure, took one of his periodic "swings around the circle" and in the course of several addresses declared that there would be no reprisals, that serenity within the party was being re-established and that, henceforth, only peace was desired, he was undoubtedly speaking the convictions of Jim Farley. Mr. Farley—being first and foremost an organization man—thinks first of the organization. I do not believe, however, that Mr. Farley's opinions in this regard were those of Mr. Roosevelt. Mr. Roosevelt is not, first and foremost, an organization man and his first thoughts are not for the organization. His first thoughts are for the Roosevelt program. And it has at last become perfectly plain that the Roosevelt program and the Democratic party are not necessarily identical. In certain quarters they are irreconcilable.

[265]

Moreover, the conclusion that Mr. Roosevelt wants peace—the kind of peace that will include his adversaries—is based upon what I believe to be a misunderstanding of Mr. Roosevelt's temperament. He could only get that kind of a peace by making major compromises and concessions. The Roosevelt temperament being what it is, I do not believe he will make them. His will is as strong as his memory is long.

His public career has not been one of give and take—of ups and downs. It has been uniformly one of ups. He has very seldom been crossed. It is doubtful if he has ever, before the Supreme Court issue, been crossed successfully on a really vital matter. He has, I think, the normal reactions of a man who has been unvaryingly successful. For that reason, he is no more likely to admit his defeat than he is to forget the men who sought to defeat him.

Furthermore, the President has lost none of his political confidence. It is a safe guess that 1938 has already been marked as a red-letter year in his calendar. I am sure that his election, in 1936, gave him no greater satisfaction than he will get from the vindication he confidently believes awaits him in the 1938 elections. That vindication can only be accomplished by the political extinction of a considerable number of his Congressional foes who will be up, that year, for reëlection.

It is from this point of view that such gestures as the picnic at Jefferson Island in midsummer of 1937, must be judged. That historic fish fry, far from being a love feast, was almost certainly the preliminary to a purge. It was the final invitation, with none of the charm missing, to get aboard what the President believes more firmly than ever is his band-wagon. Over the food and the beer and to the accompaniment of unprecedented hilarity, the last notice was given that "the boss" still aims to be boss and that those who refuse to be warned can expect to be left in outer darkness where the weeping and gnashing of teeth will avail them nothing. The Humpty Dumpty which Mr. Roosevelt now proposes to put together will have some of the old, familiar pieces left out, but the pieces that get in will all have an "F.D.R." on them.

I think that Mr. Roosevelt realized long before the last election that sooner or later to guarantee the permanence of his program he would have to undertake a major job of political reshuffling. But it was not a part of his plan to be in any hurry about it. His hand was forced, however, by the unexpected opposition on the Supreme Court issue and by the series of more or less second-rate but none-the-less symptomatic uprisings that followed in its wake.

As a result Mr. Roosevelt's whole program was disarranged. Where he obviously desired to make 1937 another big legislative year and delay the inevitable political overhauling until 1938, his most important legislative measures have got nowhere and he now suddenly finds himself in the middle of a political upheaval.

I do not believe, therefore, that either the Supreme Court plan or any other legislation is any longer first in Mr. Roosevelt's mind. I think he is aware of the fact that his next major job is not legislative but punitive. The line-up being what it is and the issues being what they are, it is exceedingly doubtful if a single Washington season will suffice to complete it. The long-time futures of both the Democratic Party and the New Deal are involved in it and, more immediately, the 1940 status of the President, himself.

It is hardly necessary to point out again that the most remarkable fact about the Roosevelt administration is the incompatibility of the forces that have supported it. No political and economic gulf is wider than that which separates John L. Lewis from John N. Garner or Bob La Follette and George Norris from Josiah Bailey. But whether for expediency's sake or by conviction all of them pitched their tents with Mr. Roosevelt. Mr. Roosevelt kept the solid South intact and, at the same time, wooed and won the Negro voters of the North. He got his largest campaign contributions from the left-wing labor unions and other substantial sums from those southern industrial areas which are most bitterly anti-union. He has pleased the radical Farm-Labor Party of Minnesota and the Dakotas without alienating the Conservative Democratic machine of Illinois. The city bosses of the East have gone down the line for him with as great a show of enthusiasm as the unbossed farmers of the Middle West. In short, he has been supported by a political monstrosity which was as overpowering while it lasted as it was certain not to last.

Mr. Roosevelt, as I have pointed out, undoubtedly knew that with such a following a break-up was inevitable. The timing went wrong. But the cracks are appearing in the right places. The realignment has begun at least a year early. But it is, none-the-less, Mr. Roosevelt's realignment. And there can hardly be any serious doubt as to where he is going and whom he will take along. It has been apparent ever since the brief passage of the Era of Good Feeling and the subsequent launching of the Second New Deal that his direction is left and that his traveling companions will be the Lewises, La Follettes, and Norrises, rather than the Garners, Robinsons, and Baileys.

The President would have had no serious difficulty satisfying the party's conservatives if he had desired to have their permanent company. He could even have satisfied them without impairing his own status as a liberal statesman. A good many of them did not relish the First New Deal. But nearly all of them were reconciled to it. They have balked at going farther. But I do not believe that they would have gone back.

That is the reason why the forming Democratic opposition to the President cannot be accurately estimated in terms of those who were against him on the Supreme Court bill or any other specific legislation. It must be estimated in terms of all those who stand opposed to the whole tendency toward executive government which the Second New Deal involves.

The number includes conservatives, like Glass and Byrd of Virginia, Copeland of New York, Gerry of Rhode Island and Tydings of Maryland, who want a respite from all kinds of experimentation. It includes New Deal moderates like Connally of Texas, Clark of Missouri, McCarren of Nevada, Burke of Nebraska, and George of Georgia, who believe that new schemes should be delayed until the older schemes have been made effective. It includes, also, such bona fide liberals as Wheeler of Montana, O'Mahoney of Wyoming and Van Nuys of Indiana who want whatever further leftward turns are made to be within the structure of our system. It includes those who have already spoken out and a much larger number, both in the Senate and the House, whose only speaking has been confined to private conversation where their comments are even more unrestrained than that of those who have joined the opposition on the floor.

But the Court fight—even though it did not give an entirely accurate measure of Democratic unrest—was politically significant because it dramatized the President's objective and also because it was the first issue on which a show-down with the President was even partially successful. For the first time it was the President who was obliged to give ground rather than Congress. The Court revolt appears to have made Congress safe for insurgency.

Between the first of April and the first of August 1937, the mood and temper of Congress underwent a remarkable change. The shadow of the White House still reached to the Capitol. But it was a much less ominous shadow. Recently the happiest and most confident men on the Hill are the President's former backers who on some or all of these pending measures have deserted him and the surliest and most uncertain are his willy-nilly supporters. This, I think, is not because the President's opponents have discovered any special virtue in merely opposing him, but because they have found it exhilarating to cut the apron strings.

Moreover, they have found that the danger that they could not survive such an operation appears, to date at least, to have been considerably exaggerated. Nineteen hundred and thirty-eight is an election year. More than one Senator, up that year and aware that the President and his Juggernaut will be on the warpath, is worried at the prospect. George of Georgia, Van Nuys of Indiana and Clark of Missouri all know that they are marked for extinction. But up to the present it is only the threat that bothers them. The actual developments have not been particularly disturbing. In fact, the actual developments seem to have revealed, not perhaps a loss in the President's hold on the voters, but certainly a considerable decline in the effectiveness of his party machine and of his own heretofore successful stratagems.

To win the Court fight the Democratic National Committee was thrown into action as no National Committee had ever been before for a wholly legislative matter. All the heralds and trumpeters were called on. Jim Farley postponed his retirement into private life and made assault after assault, in their own states, on the President's Senatorial trouble-makers. It is said in Indiana, where the Democratic and previously New Deal Senator Van Nuys had joined the opposition, that Mr. Farley managed the dedication of seven post offices in the course of a single day and made it plain at each that Van Nuy's usefulness in Washington was ended.

Back at the Committee's headquarters in Washington Charlie Michelson came out of his post-election retirement and went back to his typewriter and to the production of the war-cries that have made him famous. His words, in due time, were put on the air by the best administration speakers. Thousands of pamphlets, bearing the mark of Charlie's heretofore miraculous touch, were published and scattered precinct by precinct through the doubtful states. John L. Lewis brought in the CIO. The Labor's Non-Partisan League went down the line. An effort was made to line up the Negro vote.

But the country failed to make any very overwhelming response to all this effort. Even the response from the organization Democrats was not all that had been expected and certainly not enough to strike the fear that had been intended to the hearts of the recalcitrants. And there are well-founded reports in Washington that funds for the Committee's treasury—which, strangely enough, still has need for funds—have been reduced from a stream to a trickle by this unprecedented and unauthorized legislative venture. I am told, for example, that the Texas Democrats did not come through with contributions as they had been expected to do simply because they were aware that some of their money was to be sent back to Texas to be used against Tom Connally. And the Democrats of Texas, however much they may be for the President, are not against Tom Connally.

But there is no evidence whatsoever that this succession of administration duds and the subsequent set-backs which the President received at the hands of Congress have had a modifying effect either on Mr. Roosevelt's confidence or his determination. A minor incident, of major importance, in this regard, occurred a few days after the party split on the Court issue and following the bitter battle between Senators Barkley and Harrison for the leadership post in the Senate. On the first week-end after those two party crises, Mr. Roosevelt chose, for his over-Sunday guests aboard the Presidential yacht, Senator Barkley and Senator Bob and Governor Phil La Follette.

It was clear that—in such a situation—if the President had really wanted party harmony—the kind of harmony which Jim Farley was preaching and which would have included a truce with all factions—he would have given the La Follettes, who are not Democrats at all, a wide berth and extended his favors to such restless party stalwarts as Pat Harrison or Jimmy Byrnes or Joe O'Mahoney. He might, even, have included the Vice-President who, up to that time at least, had never been a yachting guest of the President.

The singling out of Bob and Phil La Follette, for this unusual honor, looked like a gesture of bravado or a straight-out declaration of war. That impression was not diminished any when, on the following week-end the guests aboard the SS Potomac were Harold Ickes, the Secretary of the Interior, whose status with Congress is far better than it once was, but who could hardly qualify as much of a Democrat and Governor Frank Murphy of Michigan, whom many conservative Democrats regard as the foster-father of the sit-down strike.

I think that Mr. Roosevelt has concluded that—however usefully they once may have served him—he no longer needs the party's conservatives. I think he believes that, in 1938, the country will indicate that it does not need them any longer either.

If he is right about that, then the Democratic party will be in for an overhauling the like of which no party has ever undergone. If the President is able to punish those of his foes who face the voters in 1938, one of two courses will be open to the rest of the party's conservatives. They will be obliged either to make peace with the President on the President's terms or—failing to find a haven in the Republican party—eventually to quit politics altogether. The Democratic party, if 1938 produces another Roosevelt mandate, will be the Roosevelt party, accepting, as its policies, the policies of Mr. Roosevelt and nominating, as its 1940 candidate, Mr. Roosevelt's man.

I do not mean that this overhauling can be entirely complete by 1940—regardless of what New Deal successes attend the 1938 elections. There will still be a Democratic Old Guard; the solid South will still send a largely conservative delegation to the Democratic National Convention; there will be, still, a remnant of pre-Roosevelt Democrats in the United States Senate and the House of Representatives. But the party's center of gravity, none-the-less, will have been shifted.

That shift, of course, is already partly accomplished. By virtue of the rule of seniority in Congress, a great many of the more important committee chairmanships are still in the hands of southern Democrats. But the real legislative authority in Congress is being transferred to the hands of younger men, authentic liberals, most of them from the North. The election of Senator Albin Barkley to the post of floor-leader to succeed the late Senator Robinson took that position away from the solid South for the first time in more than a generation. More-

over, the President's unprecedented "Dear Albin" letter
indicated how eager he was that that transfer should take
place. Second in command to Senator Barkley, is Senator
Minton of Indiana—a New Deal Senator, whose eleva-
tion to such influence in his first term in the Senate is indicative of the speed with which the control of the party
is being taken away from the South.

The significance, from Mr. Roosevelt's point of
view, of his 1936 success in such states as Pennsylvania
and California is not so much in the fact that it ran up
his electoral total but, rather, in the fact that it helped
along this movement to shift the party's center of gravity. Mr. Roosevelt undoubtedly believes that—from the
standpoint of the electoral votes involved and, more
important, from the standpoint of the liberalism of the
mass of the voters—the exchange of a block of southern
states for, let us say, Pennsylvania, would be a highly
desirable trade.

The Democratic organization in Pennsylvania is a
New Deal organization. Senator Guffey—the boss of
the organization—is probably the best example of the
"ours not to reason why" school of New Deal thought in
the United States Senate. He is a sight-unseen New
Dealer. This, I think, is not due to the fact that Senator
Guffey is, by nature or mental inclination, a prophet of
social reform. His New Dealism—like the political organization he has built out of it—is exceedingly practical. I do not mean to reflect upon the sincerity of his

liberalism. But politics—and particularly politics in Pennsylvania—being what it is I am sure that his devotion to the cause has not been made any more difficult by the fact that the cause pays political dividends.

Senator Guffey and his organization—with an excellent out-in-front man in the person of Governor Earle and with the backing of John L. Lewis—put Pennsylvania in the Democratic column in 1936. The combination of forces that made that success possible may keep Pennsylvania Democratic for a number of elections to come. That—since the state has 36 electoral votes—is important in any year and in a good many years may be decisive. Those 36 electoral votes, by the way, are only one less than the combined votes of Alabama, North Carolina, South Carolina, and Mississippi. And the important fact is that the Democratic vote in Pennsylvania, unlike that in many southern states, is not based on a traditional conservatism. It is authentically New Deal and Liberal.

Mr. Roosevelt's hope to free the Democratic party from its dependence upon the solid South is based upon his confidence in the New Deal control of such states as Pennsylvania. He is too astute a politician to believe that 1940 will repeat the sweep of 1936. But I think he believes that in a number of so-called "crucial" states— Pennsylvania, Illinois, Ohio, Indiana, Michigan, California—his 1932, 1934, and 1936 election victories have brought the Democratic organization to unprecedented political strength. The organization in those states, having received its great impetus because of Mr. Roosevelt is and, doubtless, will remain dependably New Deal. If it can remain strong enough to continue to carry those states for the party then—obviously—there is much less need than in the past to worry about the solid South.

Moreover, Mr. Roosevelt knows that if he manages to keep control of the Democratic organization, he will keep the party name. If he keeps the party name it is obvious, because of the momentum of habit and tradition —that the party will continue to carry a large part of the South. A majority of the Democrats of Mississippi or South Carolina or, for that matter, of Texas may not like the Second New Deal and their leaders may deeply resent the northward shift of the party's control. But when they get down to the solemn business of going to the polls, the average southern voter is likely to continue to vote Democratic for a good many elections to come.

There is, of course, another possibility in the political upheaval which is appearing in the wake of Mr. Roosevelt's second New Deal. It is possible—though, as yet, hardly probable—that the New Deal may be obliged to throw over the Democratic party, lock, stock, and barrel. I do not think that Mr. Roosevelt would relish any such move—regardless of how confident he might be that he could make it successful. He is versed, as few men, in the history of party politics in the United States and he knows the odds against third party movements. If the New Deal becomes, in effect, a third party movement, it will not be because that was Mr. Roosevelt's first choice. His first choice is to make the Democratic party the New Deal party.

Unfortunately, however, Mr. Roosevelt is not in a position wholly to control his supporters. He has mobilized and made politically class-conscious vast groups of heretofore inarticulate voters. He has inoculated them with some of his own impatience. More than that, he has encouraged them—through such organizations as Labor's Non-Partisan League, the American Labor Party, the newly organized Farmers' Non-Partisan League—to get actively into the political game, on an independent basis, to demand what—through the older parties—they are only slowly achieving. They and a vast mass of as yet unorganized New Deal beneficiaries may not be prepared to make the compromises or go at the slower pace which will be necessary if the Democratic party is to be made the sole custodian of the New Deal's future. These forces are not powerful enough to put their own candidate in the White House in 1940. But their defection from the Democrats to a party ticket of their own would make it almost certain that the successful 1940 candidate would not be a Democrat. They are the difference between the Democratic party as a majority or a minority party.

For political reasons, therefore, Mr. Roosevelt will

have to satisfy the beneficiary vote if he desires to insure the long-time future of his policies. But more than politics is involved here. Quite apart from the votes at stake, Mr. Roosevelt would attempt to satisfy the beneficiary bloc because, in general, its objectives are his objectives. The American Labor Party in New York City with Fiorella LaGuardia as its candidate is far dearer to the heart of Mr. Roosevelt—and its program is much more in line with his own thinking—than the best that Tammany can produce. The Wisconsin Progressives—and not the Wisconsin Democratic organization—are the real representatives of the Roosevelt point of view, in that state. In fact, there are few states—Pennsylvania, perhaps, being the outstanding exception—where Mr. Roosevelt is not to the left of the Democratic state organization. A third party—with no restraining conservative influences—would, I think, fit into the pattern of his thought far better than a liberalized Democratic party.

If he rejects the third party temptation it will be because of political difficulties and not because the idea is an uncongenial one. Even then his hand may be forced. The conservative Democrats may prove to be more powerful in their home bailiwicks than Mr. Roosevelt believes them to be. In that case he would be unable to bring off the 1938 party purge that is being planned and 1940 would come on apace with the prospect that the New Dealers, instead of being the purgers would be the purged.

Where Does Mr. Roosevelt Go from Here?

In that still unlikely event, Mr. Roosevelt could accept his defeat, turn the party back to its pre-Roosevelt masters and retire to the comfortable solitude of Hyde Park. But there is nothing in the Roosevelt temperament to make the acceptance of such a course a likelihood. He, I think, abhors the idea of retirement. And he is not the kind to surrender.

Moreover, Mr. Roosevelt is as much aware of the political consequences of the First and Second New Deals as he is of their economic consequences. He knows how potent the forces are which his policies and philosophy have mobilized and made articulate. He knows that if he moved into a third party he would carry with him the more militant wing of labor—and John L. Lewis. He would be accompanied, likewise, by Henry Wallace and that would mean a farm bloc of considerable proportions. Harry Hopkins would join him and bring along as much as could be kept intact of the WPA organization among the unemployed. The La Follettes and their Progressive Party would undoubtedly be a part of the new movement. So would Labor's Non-Partisan League and the American Labor Party. So would a considerable and—in certain quarters—an influential group of men who have been closely associated with the New Deal: Fiorella LaGuardia, Mayor of New York City, Harold Ickes, the Secretary of the Interior, David Stern, the increasingly influential publisher of the New York Evening Post and the Philadelphia Record, probably the entire Guffey-Earle Democratic machine in Pennsylvania.

The political force that such an aggregation could muster would be considerable. It might be permanent. It might, even, become in short order a major party and supersede one of the other two. But to get it ready and give it any chance for success in the 1940 election would require that it put a ticket in the field headed by Mr. Roosevelt, himself.

Because of the political difficulties involved I do not believe that Mr. Roosevelt desires to be the candidate of a third party in 1940. Only pressure from his New Deal following, a resurgence of Democratic reaction and his own inability to retain complete control of the Democratic machinery would force him to any such step. I am sure, however, that—much as he might prefer to see his candidate run on the Democratic ticket or run on that ticket himself—he would, if forced, enter the 1940 campaign as a third party candidate confident that his power with the voting public—and particularly with his voting public—would be sufficient to bring about his election.

CHAPTER XIII

JAMES A. FARLEY AWAITS THE WORD

THE fact that James A. Farley did not resign from the Cabinet in the spring of 1937—as he had intended—was not due to any lack of available jobs. He had a whole folder full of lucrative offers. It was not due, either, to any lack of pressure from Mrs. Farley. She is bound by no indissoluble bonds to the Roosevelts; she has no irrepressible enthusiasm for the New Deal; she would dislike Washington even if her husband were President; and, besides, she thinks that Jim ought to get into something where he can make some money.

Jim stayed on—I do not think he ever relished the prospect of leaving—because the President's Supreme Court fight was a new campaign and he was the President's campaign manager. Beginning with the New York state election in 1928 and including the fight to win the Presidential nomination at the 1932 convention —which was the hardest fight of them all—Jim has built and run the machinery for six Roosevelt cam-

[283]

paigns. Each new campaign was more successful than the last. The Supreme Court contest was the seventh. It turned out to be the unlucky seventh. The evidence seems to indicate that it was Mr. Roosevelt's strategy that failed and not Mr. Farley's. At any rate, Jim stayed on to see "the boss" through.

This, as I have said, probably did not displease Mr. Farley. He wants to make "Bess and the kids" financially independent. He would be glad to put in three or four years if he could do it in that time. But money-making does not appeal to him as a full-time occupation. He likes Washington and everything in it: his comfortable suite at the Mayflower, his air-conditioned office—large enough for an auditorium—at the Post Office Department, his Lincoln with the Cabinet number plates, the Cabinet meetings, and the newspaper boys that wait for a word from him when they adjourn, the calls he gets from petitioning Senators and Representatives, the hail-fellow respect of Ambrose O'Connell and Bill Bray, his personal assistants, even the state dinners—with tails and a topper—at the White House.

No one in the Roosevelt administration, with the exception of Mr. Roosevelt, takes to Washington and the job of running the country with greater enthusiasm than Mr. Farley. And Jim, for all his gusto, has enough essential humility to pinch himself, now and then, just to make sure that this is the same fellow who, not so many years ago, was working in the brickyard in Grassy Point, on the Hudson, and, under the nickname of "Stretch," covered first on Sundays for the Stony Point baseball team.

But other reasons than Jim's usefulness to the President and his enthusiasm for the job may have made it easy for him to stay on in Washington. For nearly ten years he has had an eye single to the fortunes of his chief. But he has now reached the age and the stature where he has his own fortunes to think about. He is forty-nine. That leaves him at least three more quadrennai of Presidential availability. But his record, to date, is the Roosevelt record and no one is wise enough to predict how the Roosevelt record will appeal to the country in 1944 or 1948. Mr. Farley's political irons are probably as hot now as they will ever be. If he plans to strike in a big way, now—that is, 1940—is clearly the time for striking.

Jim undoubtedly has given a good deal of thought to the question of his own availability. His thinking has borne fruit in a succession of speech-making trips to the country unequaled by anyone else in this entire and exceedingly articulate administration. Moreover, some of his friends are giving a good deal of thought to it and they do not hesitate to say that they have steadfastly set their faces toward Jim's 1940 candidacy. There is no avoiding the fact that Jim plus his friends is a force to be reckoned with.

But the situation is an embarrassing one. Mr. Farley

has never been a Farley man. He has always been a
Roosevelt man. He has, to be sure, never had a back
seat. But he has never interfered with the driving. If
Jim has political standing in his own right—as he has—
it is not because of any deliberate efforts on his own
behalf. The only fences he has built have been Roosevelt
fences. And that is where the embarrassment begins.
Jim, having looked out for Mr. Roosevelt, can hardly
begin to look out for Jim unless Mr. Roosevelt gives
him a go-ahead and, more important than that, an official blessing. To date, neither the go-ahead nor the
blessing has been vouchsafed. Jim holds on. But some of
Jim's friends declare that what he is holding on to may
turn out to be the bag.

It is possible, of course, that Grassy Point and Hyde
Park, although they are both on the Hudson, are more
widely separated than they appear to be on the map.
Hyde Park is aristocratic and ancestral, the kind of a
community that would appeal to the better-grade English nobility. Grassy Point is poor and middle-class: a
one street town with no front yards and with its homes
and stores built wall-to-wall with neither design nor
decoration. It is the kind of a town in which the homely
American virtues are popularly believed to thrive and
out of which almost all of America's great men are popularly believed to have come. Hyde Park's sons go to
Groton and Harvard, study law or make a "connection"
in Wall Street. The boys of Grassy Point, when they

[286]

finish High School, get a full-time job and join the Volunteer Fire Department—Wagon Company Number One.

In this case, Grassy Point did not need to instruct Hyde Park in the common touch. Hyde Park came by it naturally. And Hyde Park tutelage in the social graces was not necessary for Grassy Point. Jim was not to the manor born. But he had sharp eyes and he remembered. In fact, Franklin Roosevelt might have been much less a democrat if he had been born in obscurity. And James A. Farley might have been much less a gentleman if he had been born an aristocrat.

Despite their different backgrounds, both men had the same instinct for politics. They knew the rules. They loved the game. They talked the same political language. But there was a difference.

Jim Farley—from the days when he served his political apprenticeship cleaning up after the meetings of the Democratic Town Committee of Stony Point—has always been a machine politician. He was ambitious. But his ambition has always been of the kind that has made it possible for him to submerge himself—when the situation called for it—in the organization.

Mr. Roosevelt, likewise, believes in the organization. But his devotion to that belief is tempered by his sense of mission. When he first took his seat as a member of the New York State Senate he was quickly put down as a young man who planned to go places—preferably with the machine but if necessary without it. Mr. Farley has always been regular. He is that way by nature. Mr. Roosevelt believes in regularity, but it is easier for him to insist on it now that he is head of the party to which it is due than it was in the earlier days when he was expected to conform. I can imagine Mr. Farley as heading the party. I cannot imagine him as heading a revolt. Mr. Roosevelt, however, has an obvious taste for insurgency.

The fate which brought together two men of such diverse political inclinations and led them to pool their resources was a more than ordinarily propitious one. The union was bound to be fruitful not because the parties to it were so much alike, in which case they would have antagonized each other, but because they were so different and, therefore, supplemented each other. Mr. Roosevelt flew the ship, but Mr. Farley kept it in flying condition. It has been one element of importance in their success that Mr. Farley never has had anything to say about how or where or toward what Mr. Roosevelt chose to fly and Mr. Roosevelt has had very little to say about how Mr. Farley ran the ground crew.

Jim, of course, was for Mr. Roosevelt some time before Mr. Roosevelt was aware of it or, for that matter, of Jim. By 1928 he had worked his way up from Rockland County through the chairmanship of the New York State Athletic Commission and on to a post as Secretary of the Democratic State Committee. That year the

Democrats met in Houston and nominated Alfred E. Smith. Then, as in other years, New York was a pivotal state. And, as usual, the pivot on which it seemed likely to swing was the Democratic candidate for governor.

Jim's first meetings with the leaders of the New York Democracy were those, just prior to the State Convention, when that selection was made. The first conference was held on the train en route to Albany. There was a poker game that lasted until the train reached Beacon—an hour and a half out of New York. Then someone suggested that the time had come to get down to the business of politics, and particularly to the business of picking a winning candidate.

In the discussion that followed a number of names were suggested and, for one reason or another, turned down. Jim, somewhat hesitantly as befitted the rôle of a newcomer, finally suggested the name of Franklin D. Roosevelt. It got only a lukewarm reception. It was not until that night in the traditional smoke-fogged all-night pre-convention conference that Mr. Roosevelt was agreed on, with Alfred E. Smith in the rôle of chief persuader. And it was not until much later, and after the intervention of the late Louis McHenry Howe and, more important, of Mrs. Roosevelt that Mr. Roosevelt was persuaded, by long-distance telephone in Warm Springs, Georgia, to accept the nomination.

But Mr. Farley's early presence on what—by 1930—began to look like the Roosevelt band-wagon was rewarded, in that year, by his election as Chairman of the Democratic Committee of New York State. Mr. Farley has been a Roosevelt man ever since—with his fortunes staked on the fortunes of Mr. Roosevelt. It has obviously been a good gamble. Only Mr. Roosevelt, himself, has profited more by what has happened since. In fact, it is difficult to say who has come farther in these nine years: the candidate or his manager.

But the fact that Mr. Farley has been so single-minded a campaign manager somewhat complicates the situation when—as now—the possibility appears that he may wish to change rôles and become the candidate. In all the years of their association Mr. Roosevelt has always been the boss. Mr. Farley has been close to him. I do not believe that he has been intimate with him. Jim has had ideas of his own on New Deal policies. I do not think that the President has made it a practice to ask for them and Jim is not the kind to volunteer. As the President apparently viewed it, Jim's province was organization. Inside that province Jim was counsel and adviser. Beyond that and into the field where public policies are made and from which candidates emerge, I do not think that he is often asked to venture.

There is every reason to believe that Mr. Farley has never registered any complaint against this limitation. After all there is a limit to the number of things one man can have a hand in. Nevertheless, he is a shrewd enough politician to know that different things are required of a candidate than of a campaign manager and that, up to the present, his build-up has been almost wholly in the latter capacity. As a candidate he needs a different platform. But he can hardly get it without Mr. Roosevelt's approval and help. And there are no indications yet that Mr. Roosevelt—who has the greatest confidence in him as a campaign manager—is ready to acknowledge his qualifications as a candidate.

It is possible, of course, that Jim's friends are prepared to go ahead regardless of Mr. Roosevelt. I doubt very much whether they could ever get Jim's approval for such a move. But there is no doubt whatever that the Democratic National machine—the army of 139,000 party workers and the hierachy of chairmen who direct them—is Jim's machine—not Mr. Roosevelt's. Mr. Roosevelt, through these years, has been the party idol. But Jim has been one of the boys. Mr. Roosevelt has been a distant figure. But Jim might be on the phone any minute. Mr. Roosevelt ran the government. But Jim passed out the jobs. Mr. Roosevelt undoubtedly has a far greater appeal to the American electorate. But so far as the party mechanism is concerned, Jim carries the key to it in his pocket. The situation is highly improbable, but if Mr. Roosevelt and Mr. Farley were to disagree— a vast majority of the rank and file of the party's workers would be inclined to follow Jim instead of the President.

This fact is not due to any effort on Jim's part to make

himself solid with the organization. It is an inevitable result of his campaign technique. Nothing so thorough, so dependable or so intimate has ever been seen in the history of American politics. The story of the way in which Jim Farley learned that technique and how he made it work in 46 out of the nation's 48 states in the last election goes back to his own youth in Rockland County, New York.

After his graduation, in 1905, from the Stony Point High School—where he excelled in history and barely got by in English composition—young Jim went to a business school. He studied bookkeeping. His first job, at eight dollars a week, was a bookkeeping job. He got along, too. But no young American, out to make good, was ever more of a square peg in a round hole than Jim Farley at work on a ledger. By all of his Irish characteristics, he was a salesman. Politics was a selling job. Therefore, while he worked at bookkeeping because he had to make a living, he worked at politics because he liked it.

He married, moved from Grassy Point up the hill to a story and a half house in Stony Point, caught the 7:05 train every morning to New York, got home every night at 6:45, spent one night a week at the Elks Club in Haverstraw, several nights a week hanging around the Town Hall, always stayed home on election days and in ten years never missed a Rockland County Democratic meeting of any importance. He was a young man of "good habits." He neither drank nor smoked. He still does not. If he is an addict to anything, it is to gum and Life Savers. He attended Mass regularly every Sunday morning. He was obviously in love with his wife. He took a hand in the housework. When the first baby was born the neighbors could count on it that Jim and Bess, of a Sunday afternoon, would go out for a walk together, Jim wearing a blue serge suit, a high stiff collar and a black derby hat and pushing the baby buggy.

His political methods were as simple and as homely as the life he lived. They still are. In that earlier period, no other methods were available to him. More recently, he has followed the same methods because he does not believe that there are any better ones. His first personal political triumph was his election to the office of Town Clerk in Stony Point. He won that election at the age of twenty-two in a town which went Republican in three elections out of four. But prior to his victory he had put in four years of his own particular brand of political spade-work. And to the amazement of the Democrats, almost as much as the Republicans, he ran way ahead of his ticket. The technique by which James A. Farley helped to elect Franklin D. Roosevelt President of the United States is not greatly different from the technique he used to elect himself Town Clerk of Stony Point.

He had a great capacity for friendship. Most of Stony Point heartily disliked his political party. But everybody in Stony Point liked him. They still feel the same way about both. Jim once told me that, even now, he could probably call a thousand of Stony Point's twelve hundred voters by their first names. And in Stony Point they boast, in the same breath, of the fact that they were friends of Jim in the old days and that the town consistently goes Republican.

He held the clerkship job for eight years. At the end of that time he was not only the acknowledged political boss of Stony Point, but he had extended his field of operations to Haverstraw and Nyack. In Haverstraw, he had become a leading member of the Benevolent and Protective Order of the Elks. He was a force in Rockland County. When, finally, he was made Chairman of the Democratic County Committee it was not because he had revealed anything new in the way of political genius. He was still tall and gangling, at home with men but inclined to be flushed and silent in the company of women. He was a poor speaker and in a time of much reforming, no reformer. But, in the affairs of Rockland County, as in those of Stony Point, he was untiring and dependable. He was always on hand. He knew everybody. And his political zeal—of which he had a large share—had only one object: the health and prosperity of the Democratic party.

These were the qualities, too, which commended him to the state leaders. Al Smith—after his successful campaign for Governor in 1918—a campaign in which Jim Farley turned out the Rockland County Democracy in an unprecedented percentage—made Jim a collector of the port of New York. This was an honor, but no job. None-the-less, it was recognition. Jim accepted it, worked harder than ever in his home county and began to make friends throughout the state organization. In 1923 he was elected to the New York State Assembly.

After serving one year in the Assembly, he applied to Mr. Murphy and Governor Smith for an appointment as a member of the New York Athletic Commission, the body that controls the prize fight business of the state. This was a boom time for prize fighting. Jack Dempsey was the heavyweight champion. Bigger crowds than ever before were paying higher prices than ever before to see all manner of fights. Jim Farley took his job seriously.

But he did not retire from politics. As a matter of fact, he was merely doing the spade-work, as he had done it in Stony Point. For many years in the United States prize fighting has been the sport of politicians. This is particularly true of Democratic politicians. The ring-side at almost any major bout in New York City always has an imposing quota of the men who run the party, not only in New York State but in all the states as far west as Illinois, with occasional delegations from points farther removed.

For the big fights and most of the smaller ones Jim was always at the ring-side. He was never alone. Because he was on the Athletic Commission he had six free seats: very good seats. Because he was still in politics it was his regular custom to buy six seats more. His guests were carefully chosen. He did not overreach himself. He usually had young men, like himself, who were on the make politically. Since, in a way, the match was his show he was well within his rights when he circulated, between the bouts, among the older notables. He was dignified and hospitable. Many a Democratic potentate who, more recently, has taken orders from Jim had his first contact with him in the little courtesies which were extended to the out-of-town guests at the ring-side.

Jim, on the Athletic Commission, was dependable. He was always on hand. He made friends of everybody. In short, he simply followed the Stony Point technique on a somewhat larger scale. And it worked. In 1928 when his name was proposed as Secretary of the New York State Democratic Committee he had been so generally useful that he won the post.

Two years later when Mr. Roosevelt was nominated for a second term as Governor, Mr. Farley was elected Chairman of the Democratic State Committee and took over the management of the campaign. In the meantime, however, he had gained in finesse. His public speaking had improved. He no longer spoke hesitantly in the presence of the leaders. And he was convinced that a whacking triumph for Mr. Roosevelt in New York State in 1930 would open the way to the Presidency in 1932.

But he had learned no new political tricks. So far as Mr. Farley was concerned the New York State campaign that year was run on the Stony Point pattern.

Every Thursday night he closed down his desk in New York, caught an up-state train and returned to New York again on Monday. In the three days between, however, he had made what one might call a face-to-face tour of several up-state counties. Before the campaign was well under way he had called at the office and stretched his long legs under the desk of every important party leader outside New York City. As a result the state machine clicked faster and more merrily than ever before in its history. The result was a landslide. And Jim Farley began, at once, to take thought of the country west of the Hudson.

He thereupon entered the hardest fight of his career, to date—that of winning the 1932 Presidential nomination for Mr. Roosevelt. None of the subsequent election battles was so difficult or—up to the last minute—so uncertain as that which preceded the fourth ballot collapse of the opposition at the Chicago Convention.

He began the spade-work, in 1930, a few days after Mr. Roosevelt's reëlection as governor. During that election Jim had printed an unimpressive folder that listed, merely, the names of the members of the New York State Democratic organization with the name of the Chairman, James A. Farley, and his address at the head of the list—as was proper. There was no selling talk in the pamphlet, and no personality sketches—just names. But while Mr. Roosevelt's reëlection was still fresh in the minds of Democrats throughout the country, Mr. Farley got hold of a list of some ten thousand Democratic leaders, in every state, and mailed them, with a formal covering letter, his New York Committee directory. This was in lieu of a personal visit. It was Jim Farley, the Stony Point politician, "dropping in," for no apparent reason, on those who might later on be useful.

Jim, to his surprise, got a good many letters of thanks for that directory. Every letter, within twenty-four hours of its receipt, was answered—this time in terms somewhat less formal than those he had used before. He dug out material about the man he was writing to and about conditions in his state and gave his letters a personal turn. Within a few weeks he had a correspondence under way with several hundred well-placed Democratic leaders throughout the nation.

Meanwhile, he prepared a follow-up document, this one more obviously political. Mr. Roosevelt, running for Governor, had swept up-state New York as a Democrat had never swept it before. Mr. Farley's second mailing, therefore, was an innocuous chart—unadorned with comment—which gave the New York State vote, county by county, in all the gubernatorial elections since 1918. The most simple-minded, however, could see from its figures that, as a New York State vote-getter, Mr.

Roosevelt was head and shoulders above any of his recent predecessors including Alfred E. Smith, who was still, in many places, the party's favorite son.

That document was sent to the same list of Democratic leaders through the country with the same kind of a two-sentence covering letter: "I think you may be interested, etc." This brought an even larger response. A few state leaders began to get the idea and to edge their way, without commitment, toward the Roosevelt camp. Jim, looking over this mail, decided the time had come for more direct action.

Luckily for him the National Convention of the Elks, in 1930, was held in Seattle. Up in Rockland County Jim was an Elk of importance. He dropped in on Haverstraw and had himself elected a delegate to the Convention. There is no evidence that he took a hand in the Seattle deliberations. But, leaving New York, he bought a round-trip ticket which made it possible for him to make what the politicians call "a swing around the circle." In eighteen days he managed to drop in on the leaders in nineteen states. On several occasions he made speeches—or, rather, he made the same speech several times. He made it plain that he was out, not for any particular candidate, but for the party. When pressed he had just enough of just the right information to divulge about Governor Roosevelt. He was generally pressed. With a few leaders, with whom his Athletic Commission favors or his correspondence had put him on more certain ground, he got down to business and frankly discussed the 1932 nomination.

That trip was as good as a Rockland County Democratic picnic. He met everybody. He put himself on a first-name basis with half a dozen important men in every state he visited. He promised, when he got "back East," to do a few odd jobs, political errands, for a number of them. And he was pretty sure, when he settled down to his New York desk again, that Mr. Roosevelt's nomination was on the way.

When, at the Chicago Convention, Mr. Farley succeeded John J. Raskob as Chairman of the Democratic National Committee he immediately applied his Stony Point technique to the party organization. He established direct contact with the members of the State Committees. He had the chairmen in all the northern states on the phone several times a week. He asked these men for reports from their county chairmen and that put the state chairmen into direct and almost daily contact with their county leaders. He went direct to the county chairmen and made plain that he expected them to forward to him the regular and frequent reports of the precinct captains. The net result was that by the first of September, the Democratic organization—from national headquarters down to the precinct—was on a more intimate, daily contact basis than ever before in the party's history.

That was his method in the 1932 campaign. It was

the method in 1936. Jim Farley's national organization was of the same friendly, man-to-man sort that he had set up in Rockland County. He could not set up any other kind. At the base of the organization, the precinct captains were on the phone, at all hours of the day and night, to the county leaders. At the top of the organization, Jim Farley kept four phones busy and a battalion of stenographers (he dictates to his stenographers in groups) taking an unbelievable number of letters all of which he signed himself. He was—and is—one of the hardest men in public life to see. But, paradoxically, he saw—and sees—everybody. But whether the visitor—after waiting—has an hour with Jim or five minutes he always has time enough. Once past the secretaries and inside the office, Jim never hurries anybody. And, whether it's an hour or five minutes, everybody goes away convinced of three things: that one's own special problem is understood and will be taken in hand, that the success of the ticket is absolutely sure, that Jim Farley, himself, is a great fellow ("why, he called me by my first name and asked about you").

Incidentally, it is this direct headquarters-to-precinct set-up that explains Jim Farley's success as a political prophet—a success of which he is very proud. He explains it, very simply, on the ground that when he talks about votes he knows, better than the best of the straw-vote compilers, what he is talking about.

"Every day in a campaign," he says, "I go right down

to the smallest voting unit for the facts. Every man and woman in the organization knows that I want the straight story—not a doctored one. When I put together and add up the sum total of what 135,000 party workers have found out I know I can't be far from the truth."

On the practical side of politics—in the matter of jobs and favors—Jim will tell you that he has been orthodox. And one of the major reasons for his hold on the organization is the knowledge, all down the line, that he will be orthodox. When jobs are to be dispensed he can be counted on—in so far as he is able—to see to it that they are dispensed to the deserving. When there are wires to be pulled he can be counted on—if the question involved is legitimate and the person involved "a friend of ours"—to pull them. When he promises to deliver he always delivers—or has an acceptable reason for his failure. On Capitol Hill, even his enemies agree that "Jim Farley's word is as good as a government bond."

As for the "Farleyizing" of the government service, Jim laughs at the charge and points—with the data on the tip of his tongue—to the spoils record of preceding administrations.

"When the Republicans do it," he says, "the country is told that it's good organization methods. When the Democrats do it, the country is told that it's spoils."

At any rate, Mr. Farley has played the game with success. When he went into politics—still under voting age—he never missed a chance to be friendly and helpful. He has missed few chances since. The several thousand people—including his old Stony Point neighbors—who got picture postcards from him when he was recently in Ireland; the nearly 100,000 party workers who received letters—all signed by himself—for their part in the campaign; the thousands who receive his Christmas greeting—a letter or a telegram or a card, depending on their status—the several hundred people whom he sees every week and whose problems he takes time to try to iron out—most of these individuals feel that they are Jim's friends and almost all of them become his strong defenders. It is doubtful if there has ever been a man in American politics whose political success rested so little on fear and so much on friendship. Other men have built up organizations out of the jobs at their disposal. Jim has not neglected that. But his job-holders are also his friends.

In conference, Jim speaks his mind, with very little irritation and with no profanity. During the last campaign he professed to have a little black book in which he kept a list of his "pet irritations"—a list which, I think, included a few Democrats of national importance who proved to be of very little campaign value. But reprisals are no part of his nature or his political philosophy. I can imagine that he undertook his campaigning in the recent Court fight with a heavy heart. A fight against his party friends is contrary to all his instincts.

But the point is, James A. Farley remains what he

was at the beginning—the friendly and dependable Stony Point politician. The Democratic organization is Jim's organization because the people in it are Jim's friends. James A. Farley plus James A. Farley's friends is a potent political force. What those friends—having done so much for Mr. Roosevelt—can now do for Mr. Farley remains to be seen. Almost all of them agree that they can make him Governor of New York State in 1938. Some of the more forward among them say that they can make him President in 1940. As for Jim, he is too good a politician to make any declarations at this stage of the game and too loyal a Roosevelt lieutenant to allow himself to be involved by anyone else until Mr. Roosevelt has given him his word or has made it plain that he will have nothing to say.

Despite the potency of his political backing, Mr. Farley, as a Presidential candidate, has three major handicaps. First of all he is an unknown. The country is well-acquainted with Jim Farley, the campaign manager. But, as I have already pointed out, the country knows very little about James A. Farley, the candidate. The opinions he has expressed in his exceedingly numerous speeches may have been James A. Farley's opinions. In regard to questions of party politics they undoubtedly were his opinions. But when he has gone into the larger issues of public policy, they have been popularly regarded as the opinions of the administration.

It is possible, of course, that no other opinions will be

required of the man who is the Democratic candidate in 1940. That, however, has become less likely as every week of the first eight months of Mr. Roosevelt's second term increased the hesitation and doubt among the party's stalwarts. The hosts of the Democracy will certainly not turn against Rooseveltianism in 1940 unless Mr. Roosevelt, in the meantime, turns against the Democracy. What is far more probable is that the 1940 Democratic candidate will be a qualified Rooseveltian: a man who, instead of offering merely a blanket endorsement, does some picking and choosing from among the New Deal's policies.

Mr. Farley, up to the present, and by virtue of his position if for no other reason, has been wholly uncritical and undiscriminating in his public utterances. Whatever the Democrats might demand before they would agree to nominate him, it is certain that the country, before it elected him, would want to know a good deal more about what is on the mind and in the heart of James A. Farley, himself.

Jim's second handicap is somewhat related to the first. Mr. Farley, as head of the Democratic National Committee, has built up a very large patronage machine. It is no larger—I should say—or any different as to its operation than the machine the Republicans would have built up under the same circumstances. Moreover, the fact that Jim has handed out the jobs is one reason why he has a mortgage on the organization and that is an asset.

Nevertheless, the business of patronage dispensing—though both parties are in it—is looked upon with a large measure of distaste by the voting American public. The fact that Jim does not apologize for what he has done—and, doubtless, has no reason for apology—does not alter the more important fact that, to be elected to the Presidency, he will have to live it down. A considerable number of patronage chiefs, in American political history, have had a large share in electing or defeating other men for the Presidency. None of them has ever been elected to the Presidency, himself, or, for that matter, been nominated.

Both of these liabilities will be measurably offset if Mr. Farley can win the Governorship of New York state in 1938. Two years as the Chief Executive in Albany would shift his status with the country to an entirely different basis. He would, in that case, have state policies to determine and his determination of them would be good ground for an estimate of his competency for the White House. Moreover, two years as governor, while it would probably not impair his status with the nation's working Democrats, would almost certainly go some distance toward ending the present popular tendency to regard him chiefly as the administrator of the spoils system.

There is a third handicap which, in a civilized community, should not exist. Mr. Farley is a Roman Catholic. He is a devout Catholic. Having had, as a Protestant, considerable opportunity to observe him I should say that his religion means more to him and that he practices it more faithfully than a great many of those Protestants who would vote against him because of his faith. That a large number of people would vote against him, for that reason, is, I think, undeniable.

It may be, in fact I am inclined to believe, that the Protestant-sponsored un-Americanism of the 1928 Campaign would not be repeated if there were a Catholic candidate in 1940. For one thing, the 1928 bitterness in certain church circles against Mr. Smith was intensified because of the prohibition issue. Liquor is not likely to be an issue in 1940. Moreover, with the loss of the prohibition fight, organized Protestantism—in certain sections of the country, at least—lost a large part of its political influence. The "church vote" is no longer what it once was.

But, in the event of Mr. Farley's nomination, the custodians of America's hate and prejudice would unquestionably attempt another mobilization of ill-will. The prospect that that might happen will have a restraining influence on the delegates to the 1940 Democratic Convention, if Mr. Farley's name is presented. If the Convention should, none-the-less, nominate him, the fact of his Catholicism would undoubtedly be an election factor. It is possible, of course, that the United States has progressed sufficiently since 1928 that these defections would be offset by the number of people who—abhorring such an issue—would support Mr. Farley for no other reason than that it was being raised against him.

Meanwhile, Mr. Farley's next major political move waits upon the word of Mr. Roosevelt. Mr. Roosevelt knows—better than anyone else—that the New York state election in 1938 is of critical importance to the Democratic prospects for 1940. And no one knows so well as he the status of the governor of the state of New York when the Democrats of the nation assemble to choose their Presidential candidate. If the New York State governor were also the former Chairman of the Democratic National Committee and the organizing genius back of a succession of national Democratic victories, then his status—regardless of the above enumerated handicaps—would probably put him head and shoulders above any other convention figure. The only thing necessary to round out that picture would be the blessing of the President, himself.

But Mr. Roosevelt, apparently, has made none of the moves which would put James A. Farley in that commanding position. It is doubtful whether he has made up his mind about Mr. Farley's future or—more important—about his own. If—as his second term draws to a close—he stands in need, as he probably will, of a successor who can be faithful to the New Deal and, at the same time, hold together the party's wavering conservatives he may give his blessing to Jim Farley as the man who—through thick and thin—has managed to keep the largest number of friends in both camps. That, of course, is in the event that Mr. Roosevelt does not choose to be his own successor. If Mr. Roosevelt should decide to try for a third term, then Mr. Farley undoubtedly, would try to get it for him. But with the matured ambitions of a man of fifty-two Jim, I think, would return to his duties as a campaign manager with a heavy heart.

CHAPTER XIV

HEIRS APPARENT

IF MR. ROOSEVELT were free to choose his own successor without regard for party-political considerations, he
would probably select Robert M. La Follette, the Senior
Senator from Wisconsin. Bob La Follette—so far as I
can recall—is the one man of some importance who has,
at times, severely criticized the administration and—at
times—voted against it without having his White House
status impaired. There is a reason for this. Bob's opposition to the New Deal, on the relatively few occasions
when he has been opposed, has not been based on the
belief that the New Deal was going too far. It has been
based on the belief that it was not going far enough. His
opposition has been aimed, not to hold the administration back, but to push it forward.

Senator La Follette believes in the spending program
of the government. But he believes in spending more.
He is for the administration's agricultural policy, only
he would make farm aid more permanent and more in-

[310]

clusive. He believes in a housing program. But he would go beyond what the administration has proposed and much beyond what Congress has adopted. He is for wages and hours legislation—but he would put a higher floor and a lower ceiling than that provided by the administration's proposal. He is for organized labor—with pronounced leanings toward the CIO and John L. Lewis—but he would be more outspoken about it than the President has been.

Opposition of that out-in-front sort, Mr. Roosevelt approves of. He knows perfectly well that he is more likely to get the half loaf he asks for if there are individuals in Congress whose demand is for the whole loaf. Moreover, in his own mind, Mr. Roosevelt, himself, would probably much prefer to go after the whole loaf. Judged by what he would like to do, many of Mr. Roosevelt's measures have been half-way measures. He does not like half-way measures any better than Senator La Follette. But he accepts what appear both to him and to Senator La Follette to be half-way measures because he has practical political considerations to keep in mind. Senator La Follette, however, is independent enough of those considerations to be—with relative safety—a free lance.

More nearly than any other American of political importance, Senator La Follette is what Mr. Roosevelt would be if Mr. Roosevelt did not have a national political party to think about. That is why, if Mr. Roosevelt had complete control of the Democratic party or if a new and better suited party were created for him, Bob La Follette would be his likeliest candidate.

The story is told of an emissary from a member of Mr. Roosevelt's Cabinet who stopped in one day at the office of one of the most influential Democrats in the United States Senate. The conversation turned to a discussion of the 1940 candidate.

"How about Wallace?" asked the emissary.

"No," said the Senator.

"How about Harry Hopkins?"

"No."

"How about Harold Ickes?"

"No."

"Well, how about Bob La Follette?"

"Hell, no."

Such a reaction is no particular reflection on Bob La Follette. Hope springs eternal in the breasts of those who have entered the upper reaches of politics. When such a man insists upon the political ineligibility of almost every one else it is safe to conclude that what he has on his mind is the eligibility of himself. And such a person is almost always somewhat more emphatic in demonstrating the ineligibility of those who—excepting himself—are the most eligible.

The truth is that few men in the United States Senate get a better rating from their Senatorial colleagues than Mr. La Follette. This is not because Bob is a hail-fellow-well-met. He knows the social game and, on occasion, he loves to play it. He is a good dancer, a better than average story-teller and he can turn on the charm if the company he is in seems to merit it. But he is not one of the Senate's kindred spirits. He has no Senatorial cronies. He does not play poker, never goes to the races, hardly ever to a ball game. There is very little of the Senate's traditional and ponderous hand-shaking at his desk on the floor. Down in the Senate lunch room he generally eats with out-of-the-city guests or alone but hardly ever at the long table where his more gregarious colleagues gather.

Neither is Bob La Follette's Class A status due to the fact that there is much intellectual companionship between himself and his fellow-Senators. There is, in fact, very little. Before the advent of Mr. Roosevelt, Bob's economic and political points of view were poison to most of the Senate on both sides of the aisle. His was an almost solitary liberal—and, in those days, therefore radical—voice crying out in an encrusted conservative wilderness. Mr. Roosevelt has made the La Follette medicine far more palatable. But a good many men believe that it is just as poisonous as ever.

Nevertheless, he is one of the most widely respected men in the Senate. This is due to the fact that most of the members of the Senate—being men of ordinary but not exceptional minds—admire men whose minds are extraordinary. Bob La Follette's mind is that kind.

[313]

Moreover, most of the members of the Senate—not being of a particularly studious turn of mind—have a good deal of respect for men who know their stuff. Bob La Follette knows his stuff. He does not often take part in the rough-and-tumble Senate debates. The rough-and-tumble debating is interesting to listen to but it seldom contributes much to legislative progress. But let Bob La Follette take the floor on an issue, like taxation or government finance or civil liberties, which is down his alley and it is taken for granted that what will be said will be something approximating a last word on the subject.

When Mr. Roosevelt—on the week-end following the Supreme Court debacle and the bitter dispute as to the successor to the late Senator Robinson's leadership post—invited Senator Bob and Governor Phil La Follette to be his guests aboard the Presidential yacht *Potomac*, his action was widely looked upon in Congress as a gesture of defiance toward the Democratic conservatives. It may have been that. Or it may have been that the President merely wanted congenial company and he knew that, intellectually, as well as socially, Bob and Phil would provide it. Except, perhaps, for Harry Hopkins the President probably is more at home, intellectually, with the La Follettes than with any of his prominent supporters. I think they have about the same hates and prejudices; the same loyalties and devotions. Their opinions about the economic system and what still needs to be done to it are similar. They like action—and the forces they most like to be in action against are the same. Bob is better informed about the business of government and, I think, has a better mind than Phil. But Phil is the more scintillating. Together, they are companions after the President's own heart. A transcript of that week-end's conversation aboard the *Potomac* would be an historic document.

The 1940 campaign may have not come in for any discussion. But there is very little doubt that Mr. Roosevelt looks particularly upon Bob La Follette as a young man who, already distinguished, is still on the make. He is only forty-two. Even though a greater-than-La Follette is the 1940 candidate, the Senator, in 1944, will still be young enough to be Mr. Roosevelt's successor.

Mr. Roosevelt's blessing upon Senator La Follette would be, of course, a bitter blow for those more orthodox Democrats who have been just as whole-heartedly New Deal. It would certainly be a blow to Governor George Earle of Pennsylvania and Senator Joseph P. Guffey, his political mentor and maker and boss of the present Pennsylvania Democratic machine. It is a generally accepted fact that Governor Earle is already in the 1940 running. And it is a further, though not so generally accepted fact, that Senator Guffey would like to be Governor Earle's Jim Farley.

There was a time when these burgeoning Pennsylvania ambitions were looked upon with considerable favor at the White House. After all, the Guffey machine had put Earle in office as a Democratic governor in a state which had not had one for a long time. Mr. Guffey, in the Senate, was an unqualified New Dealer. And he spoke not only with his own authority but with the authority of John L. Lewis.

Moreover, Governor Earle had the family position and the social graces by which the President—despite his democracy—lays great store. When the city of Philadelphia—by dint of much last-minute money-raising—secured the 1936 Democratic National Convention it looked as though the Earle boom was all ready for the launching. This conviction was strengthened at the convention when the Governor made one of the best speeches delivered at that much-addressed gathering—a speech that greatly pleased the President—and received, perhaps, the greatest ovation given to anyone with the single exception of the President, himself.

But since then, on a number of important occasions, Governor Earle has acted the part of a man en route to the White House. And nothing, in American politics, is a better guarantee than that a detour will be provided. The Governor came to Washington for the President's second inauguration. He stayed at the Carleton Hotel. His suite, the hall leading to it and the lobby below were crowded with Earle-for-President enthusiasts.

In the inaugural parade, Governor Earle rode in the

procession with the governors of some 35 other states. The parade was held in a downpour. The President—it being his inaugural—rode in an open car. The Governors—and every one else in the procession—rode in closed cars. All except Governor Earle. He, like the President, faced the deluge and, presumably, listened for the prophetic plaudits.

A few months later, Governor Earle—who, meantime, had been making a great many more outside-the-state speeches than wise candidates make so early—came to Washington to address the annual dinner of the Southern Society. Here, obviously, was a chance to begin the coralling of the solid South. At each plate, and despite the fact that this was not an Earle dinner, a somewhat ornate booklet, in the flowering language of politicians who have not submitted their handiwork to the cynical scrutiny of newspapermen, told the life history of the Pennsylvania Governor with special emphasis upon his somewhat tenuous claim to southern connections. The dinner was hardly an Earle triumph.

On another occasion, following the 1936 election, Governor Earle appeared at a Washington dinner, this one put on in his honor to celebrate the Democratic triumph in Pennsylvania. Senator Guffey did a great deal of drumming up for the affair and the turn-out, in consequence, was considerable. But, though the Earle motor was running at full speed the ship, apparently, did not get off the ground.

ROOSEVELT—*And Then?*

As a result of these political misjudgments, the size of the Earle boom has shrunk considerably. Any political machine—like that of Guffey and Earle—which seems to be in a position to control 36 electoral votes is a force to be reckoned with in a Presidential year. And Governor Earle, if he manages to capture the Senatorial seat now held by the Republican James J. Davis, in 1938, will be in a place where he can somewhat repair his damaged prospects. As to his orthodox New Dealism there is no question. Nor does there seem to be much question as to his political courage and his administrative ability. He has not been a Democrat for very long. But since his conversion he has been such a successful Democrat that—given a year or two of less obvious aspiration—and he may, if he gets the President's restored approval, find a place, again, among the most favored of the heirs apparent.

Another bona fide Democrat who stands high at the White House is Governor Frank Murphy of Michigan. Governor Murphy was the depression Mayor of the city of Detroit. He, long before the New Deal got under way, laid down the "there will be no starvation" principle and made it work. As Mr. Roosevelt's Governor-General of the Philippines he did a job that will rank with the administrative achievements of William Howard Taft and Leonard Wood. But it is not chiefly for these accomplishments that he ranks among the possible successors to Mr. Roosevelt, but because he espoused the

New Deal cause in Michigan, in 1936, carried it to success in that state and, since then, has saved the administration's fingers from a bad burning in the series of
strikes that swept through Michigan in the spring of
1937. Mr. Roosevelt is aware, I think, of the debt he
owes to Governor Murphy. Mr. Murphy, himself, is
probably not yet aware whether what he did will turn
out to be a political asset or a liability.

Frank Murphy's sympathies are now—where they
have always been—on the side of the under-dog. He
first came to fame in Detroit as the friend of the under-
privileged and of labor. He is a lawyer. He was once a
judge. He has as profound a belief as any of his Big-
Business critics in law and order. If he gave the sit-
down strikers in Michigan more rope than many of
those who prefer Fascist tactics would have given them,
it was because he knew the temper of the people and
was persuaded that—if the use of force could be delayed—the need to use it would disappear. That, I think,
was also Mr. Roosevelt's belief. Events seem to have
proved that they were right and the United States, as a
result, was spared an industrial conflict that might have
reached almost civil-war proportions. Whether this
achievement will be widely enough appreciated by either
capital or labor to benefit Governor Murphy in 1940
remains to be seen.

Frank Murphy is short, red-headed, with bushy eye-
brows and deep-set Irish blue eyes. He is an excellent

public speaker but in private conversation his voice is so low as to be, at times, almost inaudible. He is probably ambitious. But one would never gather that from anything he says or hints at. I have met few men in public life who appear to be more honestly humble and who, so readily, go out of their way to give credit to somebody else.

There is a deep strain of Catholic mysticism in Governor Murphy. Strangely enough, he believes in prayer and practices his belief. And almost equally strange, some of his first and, even now, some of his most enthusiastic supporters are found among his numerous friends in the Protestant clergy.

He is not a dynamic person in the Roosevelt sense. His dynamics are of a quiet sort. But, like most Irishmen, he loves a fight and in Michigan his fighting qualities are respected. I think it is probable that Mr. Roosevelt would have given him Justice Van Devanter's seat on the United States Supreme Court. But the Supreme Court was not to the Governor's liking—not, for the present, at least. He likes politics. And, with 1940 so near at hand, I think he prefers to keep himself in a position where he can continue to be rated among those who are available.

It is quite possible that Mr. Roosevelt, if he does not try for a third term, will look around for an altogether different kind of a successor than La Follette or Earle or Murphy. These three men are strong personalities who, despite their devotion to Mr. Roosevelt and his policies, would, none-the-less, be Presidents in their own right. Any one of them, once he was in, would run the show himself and regardless of the size of his debt to Mr. Roosevelt would not be inclined to wait for his cues until he heard from Hyde Park.

That kind of a successor might not be to Mr. Roosevelt's liking. He might prefer a man who gave some promise of being as much a rubber stamp as Theodore Roosevelt at one time believed William Howard Taft would be. To get such a candidate, Mr. Roosevelt would have to find a man whose Presidential boom was almost wholly Roosevelt-made. That would be the best guarantee that, after his election, Mr. Roosevelt could continue to pull the strings.

There are undoubtedly many men of prominence who would consent to be a second-fiddle President. At present, however, the likeliest of them appears to be Senator Albin Barkley of Kentucky—who, as the recipient of the famous "Dear Albin" letter—won the contest with Pat Harrison for the Democratic leadership in the Senate.

Senator Barkley had a reforming record in his own state of Kentucky before he came to the House of Representatives in 1912. It is to his credit that, when he ran for Governor of the state in 1926, the Louisville racetrack and betting interests brought about his defeat. In the Senate he voted consistently with the liberals long before Mr. Roosevelt appeared with the New Deal. Since the New Deal he has voted consistently with that. He has not been the sponsor of any important legislation but he had a hand in the National Industrial Recovery Act and the Emergency Banking Act. He has been an unspectacular, dependable wheel-horse New Dealer.

He made the key-note speech at the Democratic National Convention in 1932 and repeated that performance in 1936. His oratory is of the old school even though what he says is in line with up-to-date liberalism. After a quarter of a century in Congress he is now, at sixty, a master of parliamentary procedure and a good man in a floor fight.

I do not believe that Senator Barkley makes any claim to statesmanship. His New Dealism, unlike that of some of his Senatorial associates, is bona fide. But his accomplishments are not a result of scintillation or brilliance but of plugging away. After eight years of so much scintillation and brilliance it is altogether possible that the country will welcome a Barkley, in 1940, as it welcomed a Harding in 1920. And it is also possible that Mr. Roosevelt—in 1940—would prefer to help to send to the White House a man who frankly recognized his debt to his predecessor and was ready, frankly, to give ear to his predecessor's advice.

The prospects for all four of these men—La Follette, Earle, Murphy, and Barkley—depend, of course, upon the ability of Mr. Roosevelt, in 1940, to designate the Democratic candidate and upon his own decision not to be the candidate himself. If the Democratic machinery, in that year, is in other hands than Mr. Roosevelt's then, obviously, the selection of a candidate will be made from an entirely different list.

That list includes such distinguished and increasingly anti-Roosevelt Democrats as Bennett Clark of Missouri; Burton K. Wheeler of Montana; and Harry F. Byrd of Virginia. If John N. Garner, the Vice-President, were five years younger he, doubtless, would top them all. As it is, Mr. Garner, if the traditional Democrats carry the day—will have a major part in dictating the selection that is made. In fact if by any chance, Mr. Roosevelt should be displaced as the power behind the party, Mr. Garner undoubtedly would step into that position.

I have repeatedly indicated that the question of Mr. Roosevelt's third-term candidacy is far from settled. I do not believe that it will be settled finally until the actual nomination is made. If Mr. Roosevelt is not to be the show in 1940, he will, none-the-less, want to have a hand in running it. That will be easier if his declarations on his own course are not too precise and final.

Furthermore, I doubt very much whether Mr. Roosevelt will decide upon his own course until the actual time arrives. No one, he would probably say, can tell what may happen to the United States between now and 1940. This country may be engaged in or on the verge of a major war. Another economic catastrophe may have overtaken us. In either event, a change of administrations might be exceedingly perilous. Why, therefore, cross the 1940 bridge before 1940?

And even though there is no crisis in that year other almost equally powerful, if more personal, reasons may work to demolish the third term tradition. If Mr. Roosevelt had been an ordinary President he could turn over the keys to the White House and move out of office in January 1941, confident that—whether his successor was a Democrat or a Republican—the Washington monument would be about where it has always been and the government of the United States would proceed about as usual. But he has not been an ordinary President. The Washington monument, in fact, a good many political and economic structures, have been or are in the process of being moved. Beginning in 1933, Mr. Roosevelt took on the job of altering our national skyline. A job of such proportions has never, in peace time, been undertaken by any American President. It is far from finished. Mr. Roosevelt, who began the project, is profoundly convinced that he, better than anyone else, knows how it should be brought to completion.

Not only that, but Mr. Roosevelt is aware that the influences which have opposed these alterations are far from defeated. These are the "forces of unselfishness and greed" to which the President referred in his campaign speech at Madison Square Garden. His desire then, was to have it said of his first administration that "in it, these forces found their match. I should like to have it said of my second administration that in it, they found their master."

It is clear that, toward the end of the first year of his second administration they have not found their master. At least, the President's program encountered more opposition and suffered more serious set-backs in that one year than in the preceding four years of his first term. If, in the Congressional elections of 1938, Mr. Roosevelt wins a less than decisive mandate from the people then it will be clear that the forces arrayed against him are very much on the come-back. In that event, the acuteness of the third-term temptation will greatly increase. The President knows his power with the voting public. He knows that no one he could select as a successor could match it. To quit in 1940, therefore, would leave the future of his whole program in the hands of someone far less fitted than Mr. Roosevelt to guarantee it. Moreover, to retire in that year with the fight going against him would look—or so the rationalizers would express it—like quitting under fire.

And there is a moral-responsibility side to this argument. As I have previously pointed out, Mr. Roosevelt has not only mobilized a vast number of voters, he has also mobilized a vast amount of hope. The beneficiaries of the New Deal—labor, the farmer, the under-privileged—have been led to believe that the good things which have been achieved are only the beginning of better things to come. They have been taken up into a high hill and shown the kingdoms of the world and the riches thereof. A little of what they have seen—precious little —has been won for them. But their vision of what remains to be won has been constantly renewed. They believe in it and they believe in the man behind it. They are confident that Mr. Roosevelt will not let them down; that he will not return to his baronial Dutchess County acres and leave them, once again, a prey to those who fattened on them in the old bad days before the march to the Promised Land began.

That argument has force. To a man who so thoroughly enjoys the Presidency as Mr. Roosevelt and who has so profound a sense of mission, it may prove to be irresistible.

If a third term President is something new to our American democracy, it is no newer than certain other departures from tradition which Mr. Roosevelt has initiated. There would be, undoubtedly, a vast amount of uproar and some serious political disruption. But it would probably be no greater than that which has heralded the other stages of the New Deal's progress. The ultimate consequences of such a major move on Mr. Roosevelt's part cannot, of course, be predicted. But neither, for that matter, can the ultimate consequences of many of Mr. Roosevelt's major moves.

Set in Linotype Caslon Old Face
Format by A. W. Rushmore
Made by The Haddon Craftsmen
Published by HARPER & BROTHERS, *New York and London*